Runes

Cover illustration   Detail of the Franks Casket; the panel showing Weland the smith at work, with part of the runic inscription above. Made probably in Northumbria *c.* 700 AD.

The runic memorial stone that stands, as part
of an elaborate stone setting, at Glavendrup, Fyn.

Runes

R. I. Page

Published for the Trustees of the British Museum
by British Museum Publications

Note on Transcription

In a general book about runes, a subject that involves several languages over many centuries, I am bound to simplify, to skirt difficulties and sometimes to express more certainty than the evidence quite justifies. From time to time, too, I am inconsistent in practices of transcription in an effort to make the material more generally accessible. In transcribing Norse texts I often normalise the language, converting it into a *standard* form nearer Old Icelandic than Old Norwegian, Swedish or Danish. There are some unusual letter forms or values here, of which the most important are ð, þ both of which represent sounds which modern English gives as *th* ('that, think'), and *j* which is pronounced like English *y*-. An acute accent over a vowel indicates it is long. Finally, runic usage does not distinguish between capital letters and lower case, and word division is often irregular, characteristics which will be reproduced in rigorous transcripts of runic texts.

Photographic Acknowledgments

The Trustees of the British Museum are grateful to the following museums and institutions for their kind permission to reproduce photographs:

Fries Museum, Leeuwarden, Netherlands: p. 27; The Manx Museum, Isle of Man: pp. 57, 58 top; Minnesota Historical Society: p. 61; Museum of London: p. 55 top; Nationalmuseet, Copenhagen: pp. 23, 29, 31, 45, 47, frontispiece; National Museum of Ireland: p. 56; New England Antiquities Research Association: p. 61; The President and Fellows of St John's College, Oxford: p. 14; Royal Museum of Scotland: p. 58 bottom; Universitets Oldsaksamling, Oslo: pp. 7, 52; University of Durham: p. 38.

All other photographs are reproduced by courtesy of the British Museum, except those on pages 37 and 55 bottom and 62 which are the copyright of the author.

© 1987 The Trustees of the British Museum
Published by British Museum Publications Ltd
46 Bloomsbury Street, London WC1 3QQ

Designed by Arthur Lockwood
Front cover design by Grahame Dudley

Set in Linotype 202 Sabon and printed at
The Bath Press, Avon

British Library Cataloguing in Publication Data
Page, R.I.
  Runes.—(Reading the past)
  1. Runes
  I. Title II. Series
  411   PD2013

ISBN 0-7141-8065-3

Contents

1
The Script and its Problems

The traveller through Sweden will often have observed, set up by way-sides, at river crossings or on open greens, standing stones with inscriptions in a curious, rather angular, script – the famous rune-stones. Visitors to the great museums and churches of Denmark and Norway will have remarked similar stones, more or less magnificent and highly carved, and there are also portable artefacts and graffiti using this alphabet. Perhaps it is less well known that inscribed objects with related scripts occur quite freely throughout north-western Europe and even farther afield.

Most of the surviving inscriptions of this sort are mediaeval, but the script's history goes back beyond the beginnings of the Middle Ages to the time of Imperial Rome. On the fringes of the Empire, and often in uneasy relationship with it, lived barbarian tribes – Goths, Vandals, Lombards, Franks, Frisians, Teutons, Angles, Saxons, Jutes and Scandinavians. All these spoke Germanic languages. Germanic is the name given to the ancestor of such modern tongues as the High German of southern Germany, Austria and Switzerland, the Low German dialects of northern Germany, the languages of some provinces of the Low Countries, of Norway, Sweden, Denmark and their settlements overseas, and (though here there has been great influence from French and other languages) of England, lowland Scotland and English-speaking America. Germanic had distinctive characteristics of structure and pronunciation which are reflected in its descendants. The Germanic-speaking peoples probably had some degree of racial identity, so it is possible, with some licence, to regard them as Germanic (as well as Germanic-speaking), and that is how I shall write of them henceforth.

It is commonly said that the Germanic nations were illiterate until they became Christian, until the Church brought to them the learning of Christian Rome, and taught them how to read and write as well as to sin and repent. But this, though substantially true, is something of an oversimplification. Some of the Germanic nations had their own mode of writing, with a distinctive alphabet called runic, each letter of which was called a rune. We know that runes were used to record early stages of Gothic, Danish, Swedish, Norwegian, English, Frisian, Frankish and various tribal tongues of central Germania, and they may also have supplied other Germanic languages without leaving any evidence surviving till today. On archaeological grounds the earliest extant runes are dated to the second century AD. The script continued in use in some regions throughout the Middle Ages and into early modern times.

Runes were not designed for writing in our sense of the word. The Old English equivalent of this verb, *writan*, means 'to inscribe, engrave', and the cognates of our verb 'to read', Old English *rædan*, Old Norse *ráða*, can mean among other things 'to interpret', used of an inscribed text. Thus, the earliest form of reading and writing known to the Germanic peoples involved incised letters. Runic script was designed for inscribing, at first on wood, and it had appropriate characteristics.

Such a method of communication or record was simple, cheap and convenient. Most

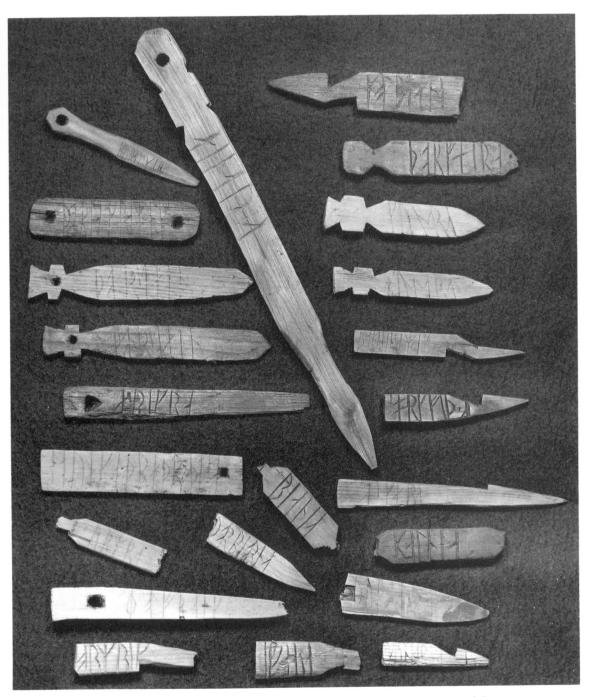

A selection of merchants' labels excavated in Bergen. Each gives the owner's name, and they are intended to be tied to or stuck into the goods bought.

Germanic men would carry a knife at their belt. A stick of wood could be picked up anywhere. What more easy than to shave a stick so that it had two or more flat sides, and on each side to cut the letters of a message? And how much simpler than the Christian method of flaying a sheep or cow, preparing and stretching the skin, cutting it into pieces, making a pen from a bird's quill, manufacturing ink from metallic salts and galls or from lampblack mixed with gums, and then writing (in our sense of the word) a text. True, there was a limit to the length a runic message could run. It would be impractical to compose a whole book on runic twigs, and they would present problems of storage and cataloguing. But for sending simple messages they were ideal. If you made an error in copying, you could simply shave out the mistake and cut the correct runes in the new surface. When you had finished with the message, the stick could serve as kindling.

No such runic twigs are known to survive from very early times or from England, for wood perishes easily in most earths. But from the excavations of twelfth-century Bergen in western Norway there have come numbers of slats of wood with runes on them. Some are ownership markers, tallies for sticking into bales of goods purchased. Some are casual graffiti with appropriately casual comment. Some, however, are quite extensive letters, like the one calling up a ship for the king's service: 'Sigurðr Lavarðr sends God's greeting and his own. The king would like to have your ship. For arms and equipment [here a passage is lost] a spear from the ?eighteen ells of iron that I sent you by Johan Øre. Now it is my request to ask you to be compliant in this present matter. And if you do as I ask, you shall have in return our true friendship, now and forever.'

Since runes were designed for incising in wood, the letter forms, in their earliest state, eschew curves, which are hard to cut in such a grainy material. Letters were made up of vertical strokes, cut at right angles to the grain, and of slanting strokes which stood distinct from it. Horizontal strokes, which would mingle with the grain and be hard to distinguish, were avoided. Thus most runes had a single vertical (a few had two) of full height, with a number of sloping arms (sometimes forming triangular bows) to one or both sides. A small number of runes were of less than full height. Even the earliest examples of the script show there were variations in some letter forms, so it is not possible to give a standard pattern for the Germanic runic alphabet. Fig. 1 is a reconstruction.

Fig. 1 The Germanic rune-row or *futhark*. The correspondences with Roman letters are only approximate. Several symbols need explanation. Rune 3, *þ*, represents the *th*-sound as in English 'think'. Rune 13, *ï*, is an uncertain vowel in the region of *i*. Rune 15 originally gave the voiced consonant *z*, but quite early in the north this developed to a palatalised *r*-sound distinguished in transcripts as *R*. Rune 22 probably gave both sounds we represent as *ng*: *ŋ* as in 'sing', and *ng* as in 'finger'. In runic transcripts the symbol *j*, rune 12, is to be taken as consonantal *y*, as in 'year'.

The alphabet has twenty-four letters, and is arranged in a peculiar order which, from the values of its first six letters, is known as the *futhark*. I write it here from left to right, but in early times texts could be written from right to left equally well. They could even be *boustrophedon*, that is, with alternate lines in opposite directions. Even in left-to-right texts an individual letter could be reversed, apparently at whim, and occasionally a letter might be inverted. Note that there is no distinction between capital and lower-case letters, and that in Continental and Scandinavian texts runes are commonly transliterated into **bold** type.

I give approximate Roman equivalents for the Germanic runes though it is important to remember that the sounds of early Germanic did not coincide with those of modern English. Indeed, it is obvious from a quick survey of the *futhark* that the letters present a different set of pronunciation contrasts from the Roman alphabet as used with modern English. Runic has, for example, a specific letter for the spirant sounds which we give by the digraph *th*. It had vowels which I represent above conventionally as *i* and *e* (nos. 11 and 19), but there is also a letter (no. 13) which gave some sort of vowel sound in the neighbourhood of *i*, *e* (what exactly it was is disputed) and which I represent here as *ï*. Runic could distinguish between the consonant group *n* + *g* (no. 10 + no. 7) as in English 'ungrateful', and the nasal stop (no. 22) which we also represent as *ng* in 'sing'.

Some of the runic forms are obviously related to letters of the Roman alphabet, as **r, i, b**. Others could well be adaptations of Roman letters, as **f, u** (Roman V inverted), **k** (Roman C), **h, s, t, l** (Roman L inverted). But other runes, **g, w, j, p**, for instance, bear little resemblance to Roman forms with the same sound value.

Where and when runes were invented we do not know. The obvious similarities with the Roman alphabet brought early scholars to the belief that the script appeared first among Germanic peoples within or close to the Roman Empire, with the implication that runes were an adaptation of the more prestigious alphabet for barbarian purposes. Early finds of rune-inscribed objects in eastern Europe, at Pietroassa in Rumania, Dahmsdorf in central Germany and Kowel in Russia, suggested that runes may have been invented in that general area, perhaps by Goths on the Danube frontier or beside the Vistula. To support an eastern European origin, theorists have pointed to the similarity of occasional runes to letters of one or other of the Greek alphabets, as **b** to *beta*, **s** to *sigma*. In the 1920s yet another hypothesis was put forward, based on the resemblance between the early *futhark* and the characters used in inscriptions in the Alpine valleys of southern Switzerland and northern Italy. The invention of runes is then ascribed to Romanised *Germani* from that area. More recently the influential Danish scholar, Erik Moltke, argued patriotically that runes were the creation of one of the Germanic tribes of Denmark, perhaps of southern Jutland where Scandinavia was nearest to Rome. It is certainly a fact that many of the earliest inscriptions known come from this general area, and continued discovery of early runic texts in various regions of Denmark make this the most attractive theory so far published. For all that, the matter still remains unproven.

Our earliest inscriptions in runes date perhaps from the late second century AD. Already they show mastery of the script and some variety of technique recording it. They are on metal as well as on wood. So mature are they that probably a century or so of runic history lies behind them. This would bring the invention of the runic alphabet back to near the beginning of the Christian era, which is as close as we can get at present.

Wherever and whenever they were created, runes soon spread over the Germanic world. By 500 AD they are found in Denmark, Sweden, Norway, England, with outliers in Germany, Poland, Russia and Hungary. They record different Germanic languages, and are cut, stamped, inlaid or impressed on metal, bone, wood and stone.

These early inscriptions are difficult to interpret, indeed sometimes difficult to identify as runic at all. They are usually quite short, often fewer than a dozen characters. Because there is no standard *futhark*, individual letters are sometimes hard to identify. It is not always clear which way round an inscription (or a single letter of it) is to be taken. Language will be archaic, and may contain words otherwise unknown. There is often no division into individual words. Moreover there is the problem of content. If we find a text written on a brooch, buckle, ring, spear-head, scabbard or plane, we have to ask ourselves: what sort of thing would an early speaker of Germanic think appropriate to write on such an object? And we have no evidence, apart from the inscriptions themselves, to help us to a reply. In some cases the answer is fairly clearly a personal name – of owner, maker, giver or something of the sort – and it is worth remembering that personal names are still the most common single element of graffiti. But if it is not a personal name, what is it?

A comparable example from modern times, not entirely frivolous, stresses the difficulty. Some bath-mats have 'bathmat' embroidered on them: some door-mats have 'welcome'. Faced with these two examples (and with little else surviving of twentieth-century English) a scholar of the distant future might be baffled as to what sort of text to expect written on a piece of floor-covering from our age. Would it be a verb or a noun? Would it give a command or a definition? Would it be a word in everyday use or (as I think *welcome* is) a rather formal or old-fashioned one. Since no word division is signalled, is it one word (*bathmat*, *welcome*) or two (*bath mat*, *wel(l) come*)? And if the latter, what is the relationship between the two elements of each legend? Today we know perfectly well what the two texts mean, but would a clue to their meanings survive in two thousand years' time?

This sort of question has always to be asked of early inscriptions, and too often asked in vain. For instance, on a massive gold neck-ring which formed part of a great treasure hoard discovered at Pietroassa, Rumania, in 1837, is the runic text **gutaniowihailag**. We can make a good guess at parts of this. The first sequence, **gutani**, clearly contains the native tribal name whereby the Goths were known (compare the Latin form *Gutones*). The last sequence, **hailag**, is cognate with our word 'holy', though probably here meaning something like 'inviolate'. But what is the connection between these two elements? What do the letters in between signify? And what implications has all this for the sense of the text as a whole? There can be no certain answer, only a balance of probabilities. One plausible translation is 'the property of the Gothic people, sacred, inviolate', but, plausible though it is, there is no guarantee it is right. If it is, it puts the Pietroassa treasure into the context of a religion of which we otherwise know nothing.

Because of this sort of difficulty, different scholars put forward widely differing interpretations of an inscription, and this has led D. M. Wilson to state what he calls the First Law of Runo-dynamics: 'that for every inscription there shall be as many interpretations as there are scholars working on it.' There is enough truth in the statement to make runologists uncomfortable.

The problem raises a question. Why were runes invented? What did the Germanic

The inscribed neck-ring from Pietroassa, Rumania, drawn before it was cut in pieces and its runes damaged. From volume 2 of G. Stephens, *The Old-northern runic monuments of Scandinavia and England* (London, Copenhagen, 1867–8).

peoples need them for? To this there are two types of answer. Some scholars, whose views are now rather outdated, asserted that the social structure of the Germanic nations was so simple, their political and commercial life so limited, that they had no need of a script for keeping records, sending messages, asserting ownership, or doing other practical things. The human memory, working in an oral culture, was adequate. Therefore the only use for such a script as runes was for religious, ritual or magical purposes. Such an inscription as **gutaniowihailag**, with that significant last sequence 'holy', might seem to confirm the theory, and the monuments record several other letter groups that look equally significant. Some early objects have on them the group **alu**, others **laukaR**. These sequences, the first connected with protection and the second with fertility, have been read as magical words converting the objects they adorn into amulets. Moreover, the etymology of the word 'rune' (Old English *run* which means 'secret, mystery') has been held to connect the script with the occult, with magic. From this type of evidence has developed the attitude that runes were essentially, in origin at any rate, a magical or religious set of characters, that runic legends have, by virtue of their script, magical properties, and that the rune-masters – the men who were trained to use the alphabet – had supernatural powers or were able to control or release such powers by their use of runes. In the fiction of late mediaeval Scandinavia the employment of runes for magical formulæ became a commonplace. This belief, that the runes were magical, attracts the fluffy-minded in modern times (just as, incidentally, it appealed to the Teutonic mysticism of some Nazi supporters in the 1930s). Our age shows a lamentable tendency to flee from reason, common sense and practicality into the realms of superstition and fantasy, and runes have been taken up into this. Indeed it is possible for a modern writer, asserting the value of runes for divination today, to define them as 'a mirror for the magic of our unknown selves' and 'an instrument to tune into our own wisdom'.

In the view of many scholars this general approach to runes is outdated and nonsensical. Most distinguished Scandinavian runologists now take the view that the Germanic peoples used runes as they would have done any other script (had they known any other), for practical, day-to-day purposes. Of course, if they wanted to cut a religious or magical text, if they wished to produce a charm word, they would use runic, the only script they had, for it, just as a modern wizard would be likely to write his magic gibberish in Roman characters. But that would not confer upon runes the status of a magical script.

Of the rune-masters themselves we know little or nothing. We do not know how general was an acquaintance with the script among the people, nor what was the standing of those who were expert in it. We do not know how the rune-master was trained, or in what circumstances he was employed. What was his relationship to his text? Did he compose it himself, or simply convert into runes the text given him by the man who commissioned the work? We do not know how busy he was with runes, how many inscriptions he would cut in his lifetime. Recently the Belgian runologist René Derolez has put this aspect of our ignorance into context. If, he suggests, there were only ten runologists working at any one time in the whole of the Germanic world, and if each cut only ten inscriptions in any one year, there would have been made, between 100 and 500 AD, some 40,000 inscriptions. We know about eighty of them. Derolez's figures are of course speculative, and there is no way of knowing what the correct ones are, but his estimate does not sound excessive considering the expansion and geographical spread of the script during these centuries. What is clear is that there survives to modern times only a tiny fragment of the total runic corpus of the early years. Nor can we be sure we have a representative sample. Inscriptions on perishable materials will have perished, and these are likely to have been the more commonplace texts, those on wood and bone. Inscriptions on non-precious metals, particularly iron, are subject to corrosion; even if they can be seen they are not necessarily readable. Inscriptions on precious metals, silver and especially gold, often survive well, though of course precious metal objects are liable to be melted down for their bullion value; but texts on these materials will belong to the wealthy groups in society and may be untypical of the general use of runes. Inscriptions on stone are uncommon (or perhaps I should say non-surviving) before c. 400 AD. For the early centuries of runic use we are working in the dark. Despite that, there remains an important, if small, collection of early runic legends which are comprehensible enough to give a unique insight into the archaic forms of various Germanic languages.

Runes were used for many centuries and in many lands. It must not be supposed that the characters remained unchanged in their passage through time and space. Local variant forms appeared, and are often diagnostic. The small k-rune, < , came to be given full height, but in different ways. In the north it developed to ᚹ, in the south and west to ᚴ. Eastern and northern **h** has a single cross-bar ᚺ; in the west it has a double one, ᚻ. In areas settled by the Anglo-Saxons and Frisians new letters were invented to fill new linguistic needs, and the *futhark* increased to twenty-eight or more runes. In Scandinavia, on the other hand, rune-masters reduced the number of characters from twenty-four to sixteen, despite the difficulties this raised in representing some sounds. The forms of many of the Norse runes changed considerably, and local differences developed in different regions of Scandinavia. In consequence, by the Viking Age the Scandinavian rune-row looked quite different from the contemporary Anglo-Saxon one, and Viking inscriptions can be distinguished at sight from English ones, even if you cannot understand a word of either language.

When we think of runes, then, we must not picture a single script or a single language. We must recognise a range of related scripts, used widely for different languages and purposes. The total number of known runic inscriptions is probably in the region of 5,000, the great majority of them in Sweden as anyone who has traversed the rune-stone-strewn landscape of Uppland will realise. Newly-found inscribed stones turn up there at frequent intervals. Norway has over 1,000 inscriptions, and Denmark some 700; Iceland has about 60, all from comparatively late times, and there are also runic texts from Greenland and the Faroes. Because of this preponderance of Scandinavian texts, it is common for people to think of runes as essentially Nordic, particularly as some of the inscriptions outside Scandinavia, such as the 30 or so rune-stones in the Isle of Man, and the inscriptions of the Orkneys, Shetlands, Ireland and the Western Isles, are the work of travelling Norsemen. Outside these northern regions, runic inscriptions are comparatively rare. Anglo-Saxon England has, in addition to several issues of coins with runic legends, some 70 inscribed objects; Germany about 60; Frisia 16 or so, and there is a scatter of runes elsewhere.

Outside Scandinavia, epigraphical runes are relatively early. In England the script died out, superseded by Roman, probably in the eleventh century; in Germany and the Low Countries rather sooner. In Scandinavia and its colonies, in contrast, runes continued well into the Middle Ages and even, in attenuated usage and often with antiquarian intent, into modern times. These later runes are of comparatively little interest, for there is plenty of other evidence for the states of language and the social circumstances they record. It is the early inscriptions that are of supreme importance to both linguist and social historian, for they record material for which there is otherwise little or no evidence.

2
Rune-names and Futharks

Each rune had a name that was also a meaningful word. We believe these rune-names existed from early times, though of course they are not recorded until comparatively late, when written accounts of the script began. From Anglo-Saxon England and related territories there are manuscripts of the ninth century and after, with drawings of the English runic characters labelled with the local version of their names. The Norse rune-names are preserved from slightly later, and at a time when only sixteen of the letters survived in use in Scandinavia, so we do not have a complete list of names from that region. No names of runes are known from the other Germanic peoples, but those of the letters of the Gothic alphabet, invented for writing the scriptures in, have some links with rune-names. Of the sixteen Norse rune-names that survive, most correspond more or less with the equivalent Anglo-Saxon ones, and these presumably go back to a common Germanic past.

Usually the name of a rune began with the sound that rune represented. To take a couple of examples. The first letter of the *futhark*, with the value *f*, had in Old English the name *feoh*. The Norse name is *fé*. Both mean 'money, property'. The *i*-rune (no. 11) had the Old English name *is*, Old Norse *íss*, both with the sense 'ice'. They are supported by the Gothic letter name *iiz*. Occasionally English and Norse runes have similar name

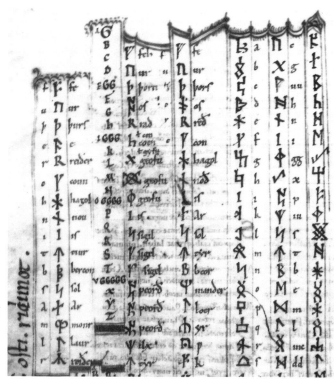

Part of a page of scripts in MS 17, St John's College, Oxford, showing a variety of runic forms and rune-names.

forms, but quite different meanings allotted to them. The *u*-rune (no. 2) is called *ur* in both cultures, but in England this means 'wild ox', in Norwegian 'slag' and in Icelandic 'drizzle'. Here the form descends from a common Germanic name which acquired variant meanings as applied in the different languages. Rarely, the English and Norse names are completely different. Rune 3 of the *futhark*, with the value *þ/th*, has the English name *þorn* (modern English 'thorn'); in Norse the name is *þurs* which means 'giant, monster, demon' (a now obsolete dialect word, *thurse*, 'goblin', is a borrowing from Norse into north-west English). One or other of these may be the direct descendant of the Germanic name.

A couple of runes represented sounds that never occurred at the beginnings of words in the Germanic tongues. Here the deviser of the rune-names had to do the best he could. For instance, no Germanic word starts with the combination *ng* (rune no. 22). The Norse name for this character is unknown. The Old English, which may represent the Germanic, is *Ing*, the name of a god or perhaps a hero of Germanic antiquity.

On this evidence we may tentatively suggest a list of Germanic rune-names and values, though there will be gaps and uncertainties. The following table reconstructs Germanic forms (which, of course, are not directly preserved anywhere). Other scholars may have individual variants for some of the names and forms, and to indicate this uncertainty I follow common scholarly convention and asterisk reconstructed forms.

1. **fehu*, 'money, cattle, wealth'
2. **ūruz*, '?wild ox'
3. *?*þurisaz*, 'giant, monster'
4. **ansuz*, 'god'
5. **raidō*, 'riding, carriage'
6. *?* Old English *cen*, 'torch', Old Norse *kaun*, 'ulcer'
7. **gebō*, 'gift'
8. **wunjō*, 'joy'
9. **hagalaz*, 'hail'
10. **naudiz*, 'need, necessity, extremity'
11. **īsa-*, 'ice'
12. **jēra-*, 'year, fruitful part of the year'
13. **ī(h)waz/*eihwaz*, 'yew-tree'
14. *?*perþ-*, meaning quite unclear
15. *?*algiz*, also unclear
16. **sōwilō*, 'sun'
17. **tīwaz/*teiwaz*, 'the god Tiw' (whose name survives in 'Tuesday')
18. **berkanan*, 'birch-twig'
19. **ehwaz*, 'horse'
20. **mannaz*, 'man'
21. **laguz*, 'water'
22. **ingwaz*, 'the god Ing'
23. **ōþila-/*ōþala-*, 'hereditary land, possession'
24. **dagaz*, 'day'

Imaginative runologists view this list with delight. They argue that the names of the runes – a magical or cult script as they think – are closely linked to the pagan religion of the Germanic peoples; so they expect them to record key concepts or features of the Germanic world picture, and to tell something of the nature of its earliest society and thought. To help them on their way, they give some of the runes symbolic or extended meanings. The name of the *u*-rune, literally 'wild ox', receives the symbolic addition 'male strength, virility'. The name of the *l*-rune is, if English and some Norse written traditions are to be trusted, 'water'; but some would prefer to *laguz* the word *laukaz*, a word which, as we have seen, is used on fertility amulets implying vegetable fertility (it is related to our modern word 'leek'). The *u*- and *l*-rune together define the two types of fertility, of man/beast and field, that the Germanic peoples depended on. This sort of approach is a good game for those who like it.

Unimaginative runologists – and I account myself one – find more prosaic importance in these names. It is clear that rune and name were thought to be intimately connected. Hence a rune could be used to express not only its appropriate sound value, but also its full name. If you wished, for example, to write the word 'man', it was quicker simply to draw the *m*-rune. Manuscript texts show many examples of this sort of thing. For instance, in the Anglo-Saxon poem called *The Ruin*, which describes a deserted Roman town, the poet laments the decay of *meodoheall monig, mondreama full*, 'many a mead-hall, full of human pleasures'. Instead of writing *mon-* ('man, human being'), the scribe puts the *m*-rune, whose name this is. To go a stage further, in the rather cryptic Anglo-Saxon poem called *Solomon and Saturn*, to save himself writing the first name in full every time, the writer sometimes puts SALO followed by the *m*-rune. A tenth-century gloss to the Latin service book called the Durham Ritual uses both *m*- and *d*-runes for the words 'man' and 'day'.

It is hard to detect clear epigraphical examples of this practice, but a classic one is on a seventh-century rune-stone at Stentoften, Blekinge (now Sweden, but part of Denmark in the Middle Ages). The inscription of this stone is a long and confused one, difficult for a modern reader to make sense of. It seems to refer to a leader called Hathuwulf, who brought prosperity to a locality – a reflection of the well-recorded belief that a good king could promote the well-being of his people and in particular the fertility of crops and animals in his realm. A significant section of the inscription reads **haþuwolAfRgAfj**, which is to be divided into its separate words as *haþuwolAfR gAfj*. The first two words are clear enough, 'Hathuwulf gave', but what did he give? Apparently the object of the sentence is represented by the *j*-rune, to be taken as its rune-name, *jēra-*, 'a fruitful year, fertility' and so 'prosperity'.

A less clear case is that of the Pietroassa gold neck-ring with its legend **gutaniowihailag**. The first six letters are generally accepted as meaning 'of the Goths', and the last eight runes form the two words *wi(h)* and *hailag*, 'holy', 'inviolate'. The intermediary *o*-rune may then be read as its rune-name *ōþala-*, 'hereditary possession', so the whole text becomes 'hereditary possession of the Goths, holy and inviolate'.

Another effect of the close link between rune and rune-name involves the phenomenon known as 'sound-change'. No language remains fixed in pronunciation over many years. The standard ways of pronouncing individual words are liable to change, usually according to recognised patterns called 'sound laws'. No-one knows why this happens or indeed can forecast when a sound-change will take place, though it can usually be explained once it has done so. Modern English spelling is so out of date that it often records a pronunciation that has long since died out. For instance, the modern 'know' shows by its spelling that the pronunciation once began with a *k* sound which has been lost in more recent times. Clearly if some such sound-change affected the beginning of a rune-name, it might also affect the sound that rune represented.

A case in point is the rune-name **jēra-*, that of the twelfth rune of the *futhark*. This originally had the value *j-* (equivalent, you will remember, to modern English *y-*). The Germanic name became, in primitive Norse, **jāra*. Some time *c.* 600 AD, initial *j-* was lost in that language, and the rune-name became **āra*, standard Old Norse *ár*, 'year'. Since name and rune were closely linked, this rune form (or rather a later development of it) lost the value *j* and took that of *a*: it is usually transcribed **A** at this period to distinguish it from the earlier *a*-rune (no. 4). For a time the early Scandinavian languages had two *a*-runes. Gradually, however, the two diverged in use. The name of the old *a*-rune, **ansuz*, developed to *ą́ss* with a nasalised initial vowel, and then to something like *óss*, with the initial vowel pronounced with rounded lips. Henceforward rune no. 4 came to be used for *o* in Scandinavia.

This principle, that as the initial sound of the rune-name changed, so did the phonetic value of the rune, is fairly consistently followed through in the history of the use of the script. Let us take another case, this time from Anglo-Saxon England. Here the name of rune 23 (**ōþila-* in Germanic) became *oeþil* or *eþel* depending on date and dialect. The sound-change involved is called *i*-mutation; the *i* of the second syllable affected the initial vowel of the name, causing it to be pronounced further forward in the mouth until it became a sound nearer *e* than *o*. In most English inscriptions containing rune 23, the character represents this fronted vowel.

In England and Frisia the rune-masters responded to another group of sound-changes in a way that makes it easy to identify Anglo-Frisian inscriptions. In a North Sea littoral region from which English and Frisian were to spring, there occurred a set of sound-changes which resulted in a sub-dialect called North Sea Germanic. Some of these changes affected the runes. In the name **ansuz* the *-n-* was lost and the initial vowel lengthened, nasalised and then rounded, so that the ultimate result in Old English was the name *os*. Following the principle I have just mentioned, the old *a*-rune should have taken the value *o*; but this is not what happened. A rune to represent the sound *a* was still needed, since that vowel remained in certain contexts. And the matter was even more complicated, for in other contexts the vowel *a* came to be pronounced further forward in the mouth until it reached a position somewhere between *a* and *e* (something like the vowel pronounced in the modern southern English 'hat'). This sound was conventionally represented in Anglo-Saxon manuscripts by *æ*. The original *a*-rune had now to be replaced by three, one to give the new rounded and nasalised vowel (from **ans-*), one to give the new fronted vowel *æ*, and one to represent the old *a* where that sound was retained. The Anglo-Frisian rune-masters produced their own solution. The rune-name *os* retained its position at no. 4 in the *futhark* (which thus became a *futhork*), but a new letter ᚩ was invented for the name. The old *a*-rune form survived, ᚪ, but with a new, fronted, value *æ* and a name *æsc*, 'ash-tree'. And a new rune for *a* was devised, ᚪ, and given the name *ac*, 'oak-tree'. These new runes have been found only in England and Frisia; hence the name 'Anglo-Frisian runes'. In those areas the *futhork* was expanded to twenty-six characters, and in England there were further additions to fit new sound developments.

Hitherto I have spoken of the Germanic *futhark* as though we know it from the earliest runic times. This is not so. The first *futharks* we have date from the fifth century; by then there is already some of the diversity of form I remarked on in chapter 1. The earliest example is on a stone slab that formed part of a grave chamber at Kylver on the Swedish island of Gotland. Presumably it was not meant to be on general view, and since it is followed by a curious Christmas tree-like sign that has no known alphabetical meaning (? therefore magical) and also by the palindrome **sueus**, also meaningless (? therefore magical), the *futhark*'s purpose may have been to summon up some sort of rune magic, perhaps to keep the corpse in the grave from getting out. The letters run from left to right, but some runes, **a** and **b** certainly and others possibly, are retrograde. The first letter is damaged, and the last two are in the order **d o** rather than **o d**, but otherwise the Kylver *futhark* corresponds pretty well to the reconstructed one of fig. 1. There are half a dozen or more early *futharks*, more or less carefully cut, more or less complete; in fig. 2 I give three examples, from a variety of dates, provenances and objects, for comparison with Kylver.

Fig. 2 Schematised drawings of the *futharks* of (1) Kylver, (2) Vadstena, (3) Breza and (4) Charnay. Kylver has occasional retrograde forms, and the letter order is disturbed at runes nos. 13, 14. Vadstena is shown here in left-to-right form, though its appearance on the front of the bracteate is right-to-left; the last rune is lost behind the suspension loop, but it was apparently **d**. The Breza carver omitted **b**, and the last letters of his *futhark* are lost. The Charnay rune-master did not complete his *futhark*.

The *futhark* of Vadstena, Östergötland, Sweden, is on a bracteate, that is, a one-sided thin gold disc usually used as a jewel and dateable *c.* 450 – 550 AD. Here the letters read from right to left, and pairs of points divide the twenty-four letters into three groups of eight. The Breza, Jugoslavia, example is cut in a piece of marble that once formed part of a church structure. It has lost its final runes. Though it is clearly early in form, there is no means of dating it precisely. The final example is on the back of a sixth-century brooch from a grave-field at Charnay, Dép. Saône-et-Loire, France. There was no room to complete the *futhark*, so the rune-master left out the last four letters.

These *futharks* show some of the variants that were to develop in the rune forms. Many variants are minor and probably non-significant, depending perhaps on the care with which the rune-master worked or the materials he worked in or the size of his letters. I am thinking here of such variations as whether a letter had a triangular or a rounded bow, or whether there is a significant distinction between mirror image forms such as ⌐ and ⌐ for **ï** (no. 13). Other variants are more important for they produce shapes that look significantly different. For instance, for **p** (no. 14) the four *futharks* have four different, though clearly related, forms. Kylver has what was probably the original, and was to remain the most common, form ⌐ . Vadstena adapts this by turning the outer staves inwards so that the shape approximates to **b** (and in consequence has to give **b** (no. 18) rounded bows to keep the distinction). Breza and Charnay have rare variants on the general theme. The prongs of the **z**-rune (no. 15) can be turned up (Vadstena) or down (Kylver), while Charnay has a double-ended shape. The **s**-rune (no. 16) has mostly three staves, but occasionally four (and in some cases even more).

Of the twenty-four characters in the reconstructed Germanic *futhark* (fig. 1), all but three are of full height. The exceptions are **k** (no. 6), **j** (no. 12) and **ng** (no. 22). It seems that rune-masters became disturbed at this irregularity and experimented with these characters to try to fit them better into the general runic pattern. On Kylver, Vadstena and Charnay, **k** is ‹ , but Breza has turned it round to ᴧ. There then developed variants like ⌄, and with one full-length stem Υ, ⌐ and ⌐. Germanic **j** was probably ⋄, but the various staves that formed this rather odd shape were juggled about to produce ⋄ and ⋄, and then again to give a letter of full height, ᛡ (Vadstena), ⋄ (Kylver, Charnay), and ultimately ⌐. **ng** was a small square variously placed, to which was later added a stave to make it ⌐.

This *futhark* – the so-called older *futhark* – continued in use in Scandinavia until *c.* 700 AD. A closely related one, but with the characteristic double-barred *h*-form, was the only one in use in the more southerly parts of the mainland, in continental Germania. In Frisia, and more particularly in Anglo-Saxon England, there developed the *futhork*, with its two new Anglo-Frisian forms. The Anglo-Saxon rune-masters used the double-barred *h*-rune, and to give the *ng*-rune full height they extended the staves of the small square instead of adding a vertical stave. But Anglo-Saxon England also created new runes to meet new needs.

The Anglo-Saxon *futhork*, as used in inscriptions, is:

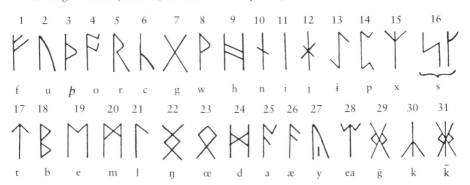

Fig. 3 The Anglo-Saxon *futhork*

Note that in transcribing English runes it is customary to use, not bold type, but s p a c e d Roman between single inverted commas. This marks the distinction between English and Continental inscriptions, and is in many ways a convenience, but in some ways just the opposite. There is also the new symbol 'i' used for ∫, while 'ŋ' is the common transcription for ⊗.

The first twenty-six runes are the twenty-four of the *futhark* plus the two new Anglo-Frisian ones. Thereafter follow newly invented runes that occur in England and are presumably local innovations. The rune 'y' (no. 27) is the result of *i*-mutation. Just as that sound-change caused the initial vowel of *ōþila- to be fronted (> oeþil/eþel), so did it affect some words containing the vowel *u*. This vowel was fronted to a sound not found in modern English but something like French *u*, German *ü*, pronounced in the middle of the mouth and with lips rounded. In Old English manuscripts this sound was given by *y*, and a new rune was devised for it and given the name *yr*, perhaps meaning 'bow'. No. 28 is a curious innovation, and not an obviously useful one, for it represents a diphthong that could just as well be given by the two runes of its different elements. The name is *ear*, which seems to mean 'earth', possibly 'grave'.

Runes 29–31 are late formations, with a strictly local distribution in the north and north-west of Anglo-Saxon England. They arose because of developments in the pronunciation of the stop consonants *k/c, g*. In front vowel contexts, for instance before *i, e*, these stop consonants became pronounced at the front of the mouth, *k/c* perhaps like the sound of modern *ch-*, and *g* possibly like modern *y-*. In back vowel contexts, for instance before *a, o*, they had back pronunciations, like modern *k-* and *g-*. In early times runes 6 and 7 had served for both front and back allophones, but *c*. 700 AD some northern rune-masters decided the sounds were distinctive enough to have different symbols. The *c*-rune (no. 6, name *cen*) and the *g*-rune (no. 7, *gyfu*) were restricted to the front values, and new letters (no. 30, *calc*, and no. 29, *gar*, 'spear') were invented for the back sounds. No. 31, name unknown, is a subtle variant of the *k*-rune found only at Ruthwell, Dumfries and Galloway.

Thus the English rune-masters expanded their *futhork* until it contained thirty-one distinct characters used in inscriptions, as well as a few others known only from early manuscript accounts of the script and probably never intended for carving. Quite different is what happened to the older *futhark* in Scandinavia. As early as the seventh century there are signs of change in the runes there; letters are simplified, adapted or simply discarded in a development that was to be completed by the ninth century. The effect was to reduce the letters in use from twenty-four to sixteen and to reshape many of the forms. This created the so-called younger *futhark* which was to continue in use through the Viking Age. But in fact one ought to speak of the younger *futharks*, for right from the beginning there were two major variant types, traditionally called the Danish (or common) runes, and the Swedo-Norwegian (or short-twig) runes. The geographical names are misleading, for the *futharks* were not restricted to those regions. Nor were they kept rigorously apart; forms from one *futhark* could penetrate the other.

The Danish rune *futhark* is:

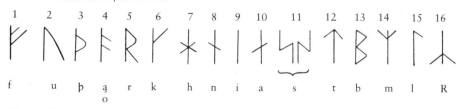

Fig. 4 The younger *futhark*: the Danish runes

The runes of the Swedo-Norwegian *futhark* are of simpler form, and some runologists have maintained that they were designed as a cursive script. Though they survive mainly on monuments, that was not their primary purpose. They were intended for everyday and practical uses, as for the written messages on wooden sticks which have largely perished. Indeed, the Norwegian runologist Aslak Liestøl has claimed that 'the majority of Viking Age Scandinavians – at least those of any standing and those intent on making their way in life – were able to read and write', and he means, of course, to read and write runes. This 'cursive' *futhark* is:

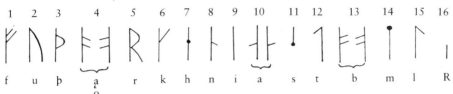

Fig. 5 The younger *futhark*: the Swedo-Norwegian or short-twig runes

There are, as can be seen, some variant forms in each *futhark*. Moreover, some inscriptions were mixed, drawing some forms from one *futhark* and some from the other. Viking epitaphs on the Isle of Man usually use the Swedo-Norwegian runes, save that they employ ᛌ as the *m*-rune.

The reduction of the *futhark* to sixteen runes raised problems of representing sounds, particularly as, to us, the choice of which sixteen letters to retain does not seem a sensible one. There are many letters/sounds in early Norse for which there is no specific rune. There is no *p*, *d* or *g*, for instance, nor any vowel-rune for *e* or *o*. In contrast, there are two runes for closely similar pronunciations of *a* (distinguished as **a** and **ạ**), and there are two types of *r*-rune (**r**, **R**). In consequence, runic spelling in the Viking Age is precarious.

If you wished to commemorate a king (which in standard Old Norse is *konungr*), you would have to spell the title **kunukr** or **kunukR** (with *n* omitted before *g*, and **k** used in place of the non-existent *g*-rune). The word *dróttinn*, 'prince, lord', would have to be represented **trutin**. A man called Ófeigr would appear on his grave-stone as **ufaikR**. If someone was killed at Upsala, his epitaph would have to say it happened at **ubsalum**.

It is alleged that foreigners spell better than they pronounce; but it took the Vikings a couple of centuries or so before they realised their spelling system needed improvement, and for this the script needed change and expansion. One sound-change helped. The rune-name *ạ́ss* became *óss*. Henceforward rune no. 4 could stand for *o*. Two new vowel runes were created, ᚧ to represent *æ* and ᛁ for *e*. Then new consonant runes were invented to represent the stop consonants, *p*, *d* and *g*. These were formed by adding dots to existing rune forms; dotted **k** ᚴ gave *g*, dotted **t** ᛏ gave *d*, and, reversing the pattern, dotted **b** ᛒ gave *p*. By now the Roman alphabet was beginning to be used in Scandinavia – it first appeared in Denmark on the coins of King Sveinn Forkbeard who ruled *c.* 985–1014. More and more, runes were affected by Roman. New characters were devised to correspond with Roman letters which hitherto had had no runic parallel simply because mediaeval Norse did not need them. So, runes for *q*, *x*, *z* appeared, and the *futhark* order was replaced by that of the alphabet. But by this time runes were in decline.

Even when you know the values of the characters of the *futhark* at any time, there are still things in the writing system that need explanation. For instance, runes can be ligatured. Two, three or even more letters could be combined, perhaps to save space or improve the layout of a text. Such ligatures are called bind-runes. Instead of cutting **ga**, the rune-master can bind the two ᛉ, transcribed **g͡a**. Instead of **aR** he could put ᛉ, **a͡R**. An English rune-master, writing the word 'help', could begin it ᚻᛏ, 'h͡e͡l'.

There are also spelling peculiarities. A repeated letter (or even a group of letters) need not be repeated in a runic text. Double consonants, for instance, are usually represented as single (at any rate outside England), and this even applies when the same consonant ends one word and begins the next. We have seen the Pietroassa neck-ring text **wihailag**, and noted that it can be identified as *wih hailag* with the *h*-rune doing double duty. More striking is the Viking stone from Väsby, Uppland, Sweden, where the owner ordered the inscription **alit raisa stain þin oftiR sik sialfan hon toknuts kialt anklanti**. Written out in full this would be *Ali lit raisa stain þin oftiR sik sialfan. Hon tok Knuts kialt a Anklanti*, 'Áli had this stone put up in his own honour. He took Knútr's payment of *danegeld* in England.' There are three distinct cases of runes being used twice over.

A second characteristic affects the nasal consonants *n* and *m*. They can be omitted in spelling if they precede what are called homorganic stop consonants: in practice this means that *m* can be missed out before *p* or *b*, and *n* before *t, d, k, g*. Thus, **kabu** can stand for **kambu*, 'comb', and the personal name **WiduhundaR* appear as **widuhudaR**.

Finally, runic inscriptions do not always note word division. Sometimes they do, sometimes not. Sometimes they note it in part of an inscription, but not the whole. So, the bracteate inscription, **ekfakaRf**, at first sight not meaningful, can properly be divided (and the last word expanded to a form recorded elsewhere), *ek FakaR f(ahido)*, 'I, FakaR, inscribed (this)'. One maker's formula, **hagiradaR:tawide**, 'HagiradaR made (this)', has its subject and verb nicely distinguished; another, **bidawarijaRtalgidai**, 'BidawarijaR cut (this inscription)', doesn't.

With all this under our belt, we can now get on to looking at some inscriptions.

3
The Early Inscriptions

The earliest runic inscriptions identified so far are from *c.* 200 AD or perhaps a little later. At that date runes were concentrated in the north, and used on portable objects of metal, wood and bone. Excavations of bogland sites in Schleswig (North Germany), Fyn, Sjælland and Jylland (Denmark) and Skåne (Sweden, mediaeval Denmark) have produced masses of artefacts. The concentration of finds suggests they were sacrificial deposits, perhaps of war-booty, made at sites of cult importance over some centuries. The number of runic objects is of course minimal in comparison with the total deposits, so that a few new finds may make disproportionately large and important changes in the material available to the runologist.

This was demonstrated in the 1970s and 1980s, as finds excavated at Illerup bog, near Skanderborg, Jylland, were being processed, cleaned and conserved. Runes were noticed on shield-mounts, spear-heads and a wooden plane. The first one spotted, on the bronze mount of a shield grip, simply said **swarta**. This is presumably the owner's name, Swarta, the black one. More recently two silver mounts from shields were also found to have runes on them. One is a maker's formula, **niþijo tawide**, 'Nithijo made (this)'; the other has what seems to be a personal name, **laguþewa**. The plane has the legend **afilaiki**, which also is taken to be a personal name. Of these inscriptions, those on the bronze mount and on the plane are cut from left to right; those on the silver mounts are from right to left. On two spear-heads there are texts identical in content though produced by different methods; one is incised in the usual way but the other is die-stamped. These were originally read from left to right, **ojingaR**, interpreted as a personal name. More recently they have been read from right to left, **wagnijo**, also identified as a personal name.

Sceptical readers will pause here, wondering what credence they can give to experts who read a text from left to right or from right to left at will, and still manage to get

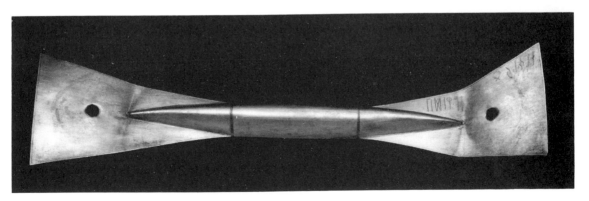

One of the silver shield-mounts from Illerup bog, Jylland. The runes, curiously placed and reading right to left, give the maker's name.

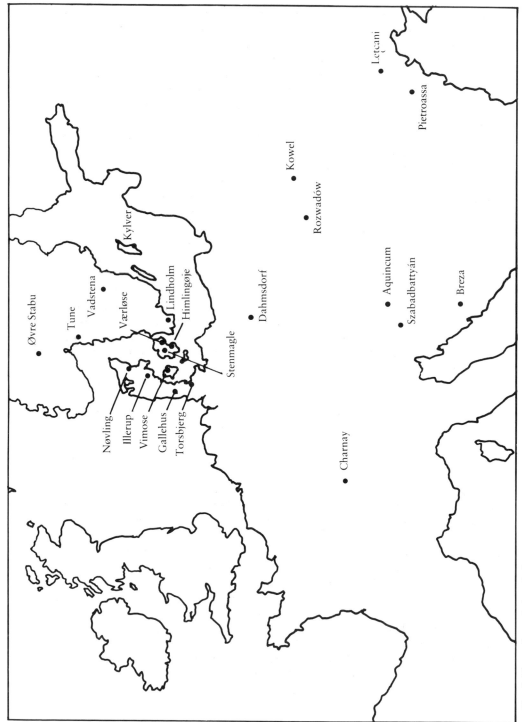

Fig. 6 The early runic inscriptions.

some sense out of it. Their credulity will be further strained to learn that some of these texts need emendation to produce proper forms: in the case of **laguþewa(R)**, the runologist has to assume an error, loss of the inflexional ending *-R*, and the same probably applies to **afilaiki(R)**. Indeed in interpreting runic inscriptions we so often detect error that we question the competence of the rune carvers: the Danish runologist, Erik Moltke, in particular has argued that many of the smiths who cut inscriptions in metal objects may have been semi-literate, with only partial understanding of their runes.

The inscriptions examined so far are sparse, and show regrettable poverty of content. All contain personal names. While *Swarta* is a perfectly likely one – after all, people are still called Black – the others are more speculative, and have to be constructed from our knowledge of the principles of Germanic name-giving.

On the other hand, these inscriptions give important information. They are early, and they show that by 200 AD runes were already skilfully used. Indeed, the Illerup spear-maker was sophisticated enough to have cut a die with, presumably, his trade name on it to stamp his wares with.

Some of the Illerup finds have archaeological links with other parts of the north, and indeed if they are war-booty we would expect them to have originated some distance from Illerup. By *c*. 200 AD, then, runes may have been quite widely scattered. Certainly there are roughly contemporary texts from elsewhere in Denmark. From Vimose, Fyn, is a plane with a number of runic sequences on it, all of them uncertain of meaning save the group **talijo**, 'plane'. Vimose also produced a bone comb with the personal name **harja**, and a copper-alloy saddle-buckle with the text, hidden when it was worn, **aadagasu laasauwija**; this, being incomprehensible, is thought to be magical. There is also from Vimose a scabbard-chape with inscriptions on both sides, one of which reads **makija**, 'sword'.

From Torsbjerg/Thorsberg, Schleswig, comes a second scabbard-chape also with two inscriptions, one recording a personal name **owlþuþewaR**. Further afield still, from a grave-mound at Øvre Stabu, Opland, Norway, there is a spear-head with a runic text hatched across the blade. This time it seems to give the weapon's name, **raunijaR**, 'tester'.

To about the same date is attributed a group of brooches, probably women's, of different types. There is a very early specimen from Meldorf, Süderdithmarschen, North Germany, apparently from the first century AD. A few rune-like characters are engraved on it, which some (but not all) runologists regard as the earliest surviving evidence for runic writing. More clearly convincing as runes are the letters on a series of slightly later brooches. From a woman's grave at Himlingøje, Sjælland, comes a bow fibula with a damaged legend, of which can be read **widuhudaR**, possibly the rune-master's name. A woman's grave at Værløse, Copenhagen, yielded a brooch with the legend **alugod**, which looks like a female name. A runic brooch found at Nøvling, Jylland, has two words, not divided as such, and here we can actually identify a sentence, albeit a short one: **bidawarijaR talgidai**, 'BidawarijaR carved (these runes)'. Among the grave-goods of a woman's burial at Gårdlösa, Skåne, was a brooch with a roughly scratched text, probably incomplete, **ekunwod(iR)**, 'I, UnwodiR, (cut these runes)'. To the modern reader these brooch texts reveal a curious sense of priorities: their tendency to name not the owner or the giver of the jewel, but the rune-master, the man who cut the runes.

Believers in rune-magic explain this. The rune-master is here recording his control over the script and therefore over the magic it embodies. The piece of jewellery has become an amulet.

In the next few centuries the script spread far beyond the north, accompanying the various Germanic-speaking peoples in their travels and settlements in Europe. There is a small group of inscriptions on spear-heads which archaeologists date to the third century AD. Their runes are formed in silver inlay in the blades, and are usually accompanied by decorative or symbolic designs in the same technique. One from Dahmsdorf, East Germany, reads **ranja**. This gives the weapon-name, perhaps 'the one that makes them run' or 'stabber'. Similar is the name on the spear-head picked up at Kowel, USSR (formerly Poland): **tilarids**, 'attacker'. A third example, of different form, comes from a cremation grave at Rozwadów, Poland; it is hard to give any sense to its runes.

The fourth century saw runes established farther south. There are two pieces of that date in Rumania. One is the Pietroassa neck-ring which, the inscription indicates, is Gothic. The other is a more lowly everyday object, a spindle-whorl of baked clay found at Leṭcani. Before firing it had runes cut in its surface. Apparently they give an owner formula and perhaps the giver's name *Rango*, though why such an insignificant object should have such texts I do not know. In Hungary too there is a fifth-century silver brooch from Szabadbattyán, with six runes set in two groups, **marŋ sd**. From this has been deduced a personal name *Maring*, which would be south Germanic, or *Marings*, which is Gothic. From a century later come a couple of inscriptions found at Bezenye, also in Hungary. They are on the backs of a pair of matched silver brooches that formed part of the grave-goods in a Lombardic woman's grave. Each inscription consists of two words set back to back: **godahid⏐unja** and **karsiboda⏐segun**. These have been taken as two sentences addressed by the givers of the brooches to their new owner. 'Godahild (wishes) joy.' 'I Arsiboda (wish) blessing.' This elliptical way of expressing things looks pretty dubious to a newcomer to runes, but there are parallel examples in other early inscriptions.

From this general area of the south-east come two *futhark* inscriptions, both tentatively attributed to the sixth century. One is from the ruins of a Byzantine church building at Breza, near Sarajevo, Jugoslavia. On a stone that formed part of a marble pillar a passer-by has casually cut a *futhark*. The last three letters are broken away, and the carver carelessly missed out **b**, so what remains is **fuþarkgwhnijïpxsteml**. The other example is on the back of a silver-gilt brooch which was part of a treasure hoard dug up at Aquincum, near Budapest, Hungary. There are two texts, one of very uncertain import, the other **fuþarkgw**. We can hardly assume that this is just a casual graffito, and the shortened Aquincum *futhark* must be seen in the context of other *futharks* on portable objects such as brooches and bracteates. The concept of rune-magic is usually brought in to explain these. The total power of the runes in the alphabet is being applied to secure or defend the wearer of the jewel.

This seems to represent the end of runes in the south-east of Europe. The period of the fifth to seventh centuries shows them in quite common use in central Germany; then, with the coming of Christianity, runes disappear. The German inscriptions present the dialects of various early Germanic tribes, Alemanni, Franks, perhaps Angles and Burgundians, while the latest of them suggests the sound-changes that were to produce Old

High German. The runes are mainly on brooches, though there are also texts on two or three little boxes, a buckle, an amber bead, a belt-fitting, a couple of sword-blades and a spear-head. Interpretation is difficult, sometimes impossible. Easiest, of course, is to assume that many of them give personal names, and sometimes this is certain, as **husibald** on a sword-blade found at Steindorf, Oberbayern, **idorih** on a spear-head from Wurmlingen, Württemberg, and **þuruþhild** on a disc-brooch from Friedberg, Hessen. Sometimes it is less clear, as the ?women's names **rada:daþa** on a brooch from Soest, Westphalia. Occasionally there is a perfectly comprehensible statement: **boso:wraetruna**, 'Boso wrote runes' on the Freilaubersheim, Rheinland-Pfalz, brooch. But more often there are letter sequences which are quite pronounceable and so are to be assumed meaningful, but where we now cannot be sure what they meant. One of the German inscriptions gives a glimpse into a lost world of paganism. This is one of the two runic brooches taken from the cemetery at Nordendorf, near Augsburg. It has four lines of runes, one of which, **awaleubwini**, is simply two personal names, *Awa* and *Leubwini*. The other three lines seem to name three pagan gods. Two of them, **wodan** (= Old English *Woden*), **wigiþonar** (= 'Hallowed Thor'), are known from other Germanic sources. The third is **logaþore**, perhaps equivalent to an obscure Old Norse god called *Lóðurr*.

It is reasonable to deduce that the evidence of time and place here shows runic script spreading from a base in the north to the south and east. This is partly the effect of the movement of peoples, such as the Goths who travelled through Europe; but partly it is due, I think, to cultural contacts between different Germanic peoples. One further area of the Continent has runes – the Low Countries – but here it is more difficult to trace development because of peculiarities of the Anglo-Frisian/North Sea Germanic runes that I have listed already.

The earliest runic texts from Frisia yet found are from the sixth century. There are two gold coins, *solidi*, imitations of Roman prototypes but with runic legends. One, from Harlingen, has **hada**, clearly a man's name, perhaps that of the moneyer, the other, from Schweindorf, Ostfriesland, reads **weladu**, probably for *Welandu*, also a masculine personal name form. These two are, however, not the most significant of inscriptions from the region. During the Dark Ages many Frisians lived on artificial mounds, called *terpen*, raised above the surrounding waterlogged countryside. In recent decades these mounds have been dug into and have produced important archaeological finds. The earth of the mounds is congenial to the survival of organic materials, notably wood. Hence from Frisia we know a comparatively large number of inscriptions on this material, which, it will be remembered, is the material for which runes were designed.

A gold *solidus* found at Harlingen, Frisia, with a runic legend naming a man Hada.

Bone as well as wood is well preserved in Frisia, so we have a group of everyday objects, combs, weaving-slays, with texts on them. Readers will scarcely be surprised to learn that some of these inscriptions are inadequately interpreted, while others have the dull content of personal names. A certain example of the latter is a yew-wood weaving-slay from Westeremden, roughly dated 550–750 AD, with the inscription **adugislu: mᵇgisuhldu**, 'for Adugisl and Gisuhild', presumably the owners, man and wife, of this piece of equipment. A bone comb from Amay, of roughly similar date, has **eda**, which again could be a man's name. On the other hand, another bone comb of rather later date, from Toornwerd, has simply **kobu**, which just means 'comb', in case anyone couldn't work out what it was intended to be. A combination of the two types is on a comb (of which only the back-plates remain) from Oostum. One plate has **... kabu**, the other **deda habuku**: '.... comb', 'Habuku made (it).' If these seem too pedestrian, you may be cheered by a wooden stick, rather like a weaving-slay in form, from Westeremden, that has a legend so long and obscure that it is described as magic. But then, even the authenticity of this object has been questioned.

Though in these early centuries runes spread far afield, Scandinavia remained the heartland. There the script was used on a variety of objects, some splendid, some commonplace, some extraordinary. Splendid was a great horn made of gold, found by chance near the village of Gallehus, Tønder, Jylland, in 1734. It was one of a pair, for a

One of the two gold horns found at Gallehus, Jylland, now lost and shown here from an early engraving. This one has a maker's formula cut round the brim.

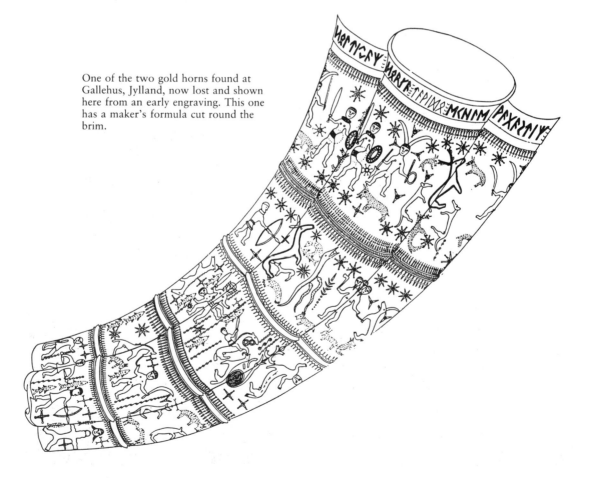

similar horn was discovered nearby nearly a century earlier. The 1734 horn was distinctive in having, as well as a variety of animal and human figure decorations, a runic inscription round the top. This magnificent treasure was sent to the royal collection, whence it was stolen in 1802 and melted down, so it and its runes survive only in early reproductions. Luckily these are clear: the text said, **ekhlewagastiR:holtijaR: horna:tawido**, 'I, Hlewagastir, son of Holti, made the horn.' Commonplace is a small wooden box of roughly the same date, found in a peat-bog at Stenmagle, Sjælland. This has a similar message: **hagiradaR:tawide**, 'HagiradaR made (this).' Extraordinary is an object of no obvious practical purpose, found at Lindholm, Skåne, and dated about a century later. This is a piece of bone carved into a roughly fish-like shape and with runes cut on two of its three surfaces. One side has the rune-master's name: **ekerilaRsawilagaRhateka**, 'I, an ErilaR [a title, or an office], am called SawilagaR.' The other side has a sequence of runes which must arouse curiosity: **aaaaaaaaRRRn-nn?bmuttt:alu**. Obviously this is not plain language, and since it ends with the well-attested magical word **alu**, it is natural to take the whole lot as magical gibberish, and to identify this chunk of bone as an amulet of some sort. The title and name of the rune-master may then add to the power of the magic: it shows it was produced by a man of authority.

For many years, until, say, the eighth century, the older *futhark* continued in use on a range of objects in all three Scandinavian lands: on brooches, a gold neck-ring, a bronze

Above The small wooden box from the peat-bog at Stenmagle, Sjælland.

Below Detail (inverted) showing the maker's inscription.

statuette of a male figure, a whetstone, bone scrapers for dressing skins, a spear-shaft, a bone knife-handle and so on. During this period, however, there were two important developments: i) runes on bracteates, thin gold discs stamped with designs derived from Imperial Roman coins and used as pendants or ornaments, and ii) rune-stones.

There is some disagreement about the dating of the bracteates. The Dane Erik Moltke has recently asserted that 'if we assign the runic bracteates to *c.* AD 500 ± 50 years, we are probably not far wrong.' There are large numbers of bracteates – over five hundred distinct stamps are recognised – and of them somewhere near a third have runes. The centre of distribution seems to be Denmark. Unfortunately, though the number of runic bracteates is large, the number with intelligible inscriptions is small. Often it is clear that inscriptions have been garbled by the craftsman, and sometimes he seems to have put runes (or something like runes) on his work at random, knowing that every decent bracteate had an inscription but being himself illiterate.

For all that, there are inscription types that can be distinguished. Some bracteates have well-known magical words, like **alu, auja, laþu** and **laukaR**, or variants or abbreviations of them, as **al, lkaR, lauR, lþu**. There are other apparently meaningless or rhyming groups on bracteates that may also be magic: **salusalu** or **luwatuwa**. In all these cases the inscription converts the bracteate into an amulet. There are bracteates that have complete or part *futharks*, and these are often assumed to be charms also. There are rune-master formulae in which the writer of the runes names himself (as on the Lindholm amulet). So, **hariuhahaitika:farauisa:gibuauja**: 'I am called Hariuha: the one wise to danger: *gibu auja*, I give good luck.' Or **ikakaRfahi**, 'I, AkaR, write.' Here the man's name reinforces the charm.

The rune-stones are something very different and ultimately more important, for they are the first examples of a memorial type that was to continue into the Middle Ages and to provide essential evidence of language, history, political events and social conditions. Dating is uncertain in the early period for there is often little to go on but the forms of the runes and of the language, and these are notoriously imprecise bits of evidence. The earliest stones seem to be the Norwegian, and then the Swedish, with the custom of raising rune-stones reaching Denmark only at the end of the older *futhark* period, say the beginning of the eighth century.

Rune-stones have some textual similarities with the amulet bracteates, suggesting that runes on memorial and grave-stones sometimes had a magical purpose – to keep the grave from desecration or the corpse in the grave. A stone from a grave-mound at Elgesem, Vestfold, Norway, has simply **alu**. There are stones with rune-master formulae, as that of Järsberg, Värmland, Sweden. Its confused lines of runes running in different directions have been sorted out to read: **ubaRhite:harabanaR hait ekerilaR runoRwaritu**, 'UbaR I am called. HrabnaR I am called. I, the ErilaR, wrote (these) runes.' Sometimes runes are called 'god-descended' or 'glorious', which also suggests supernatural power in their use.

More obvious memorial stones are those with single names, presumably the dead, on them. Sometimes the name will be in the possessive, as **keþan**, 'Keþa's (stone, grave)' (Belland, Vest-Agder, Norway). More explicit is **hnabudashlaiwa**, 'Hnabud's grave-mound' (Bø, Rogaland, Norway) or **hAriwulfs.stAinaR**, 'Hariwulf's stones' (Rävsal, Bohuslän, now Sweden, but mediaeval Norway). Then there are the full-scale memorials, sometimes in verse, as:

Ek Wiwar after Woduride
witandahalaiban worahto r(unor)

'I, Wiwar, in memory of Wodurid, guardian of the bread, made (these) runes.' The title 'guardian of the bread' may sound odd to us, but we should remember that our modern word 'lord' derives from Old English *hlaford*, which even earlier was **hlaf-ward* (= loaf-ward). This commemoration text, on a stone from Tune, Østfold, Norway, continues with a rather dark saying referring to inheritance (and in this anticipates some of the Viking Age rune-stones).

Towards the end of this early period, say *c.* 700 AD, rune-stones appear for the first time on Danish territory, in Blekinge, now part of Sweden. Here is a group of four stones whose importance is far greater than their numbers would suggest. They are from Stentoften, Björketorp, Istaby and Gummarp, the last known only from early accounts since it does not survive. Björketorp stands on its original site, forming a complex with two other, uninscribed, standing stones. Stentoften also may once have been part of a greater monument. The Istaby inscription is comprehensible; it gives the earliest extant Danish commemoration text: 'In memory of HariwulafR, HaþuwulafR, son of Haeru-wulafR, cut these runes.' The same family (presumably) was recorded on the Gummarp and Stentoften stones. Gummarp said cryptically that 'HaþuwolafR set three

staves (runic letters)' and then gives the three staves he set, **fff**. These must, it is believed, have served some magical purpose. Stentoften has an intricate and complex inscription which mentions HariwolafR and HaþuwolafR, implies a control of hidden forces through rune magic, and invokes a curse on *sa þat bariutiþ*, 'he who breaks (this monument)'. Björketorp has a similar curse and again speaks of runes full of might, but does not name any names.

Something odd was going on in this corner of Denmark, and imaginative runologists speculate fiercely on what it was. It is a relief to turn to the unimaginative ones who ascribe the importance of these stones to their language forms and runic types. They suggest new and far-reaching developments. The language shows the first changes from a primitive Norse towards Old Danish, and the runes indicate that the older *futhark* was becoming obsolete.

The Istaby, Blekinge, rune-stone, probably the oldest surviving Danish memorial stone.

4
Anglo-Saxon Runes

Germanic tribes came to England in force in the fifth century AD, and it is sensible to think they brought runes with them. Since English runes have common characteristics with Frisian ones, and since these reflect sound-changes characteristic of both early English and Frisian, it is natural to conclude that the English runes came here from the nearest point on the North Sea littoral, Frisia/Friesland. But things were probably not as simple as that. The Germanic invaders of England comprised a variety of peoples, and may have brought a variety of runes with them, though it was to be the Anglo-Frisian ones that predominated.

Fig. 7 the Caistor-by-Norwich runes.

A test case is the earliest runic inscription known in England, which comes from the great cremation cemetery at Caistor-by-Norwich, Norfolk. It dates from *c.* 400 and is on a roe-deer's ankle-bone found in one of the burials and probably used as a playing-piece. Its text reads **raïhan** which seems to mean, reasonably enough, 'roe-deer', but the importance of the inscription is partly in its early date (in theory before the Anglo-Saxon invasions of England began) and partly in its form of the *h*-rune, which is the northern ᚺ , not the Anglo-Frisian shape, ᚻ . The incomers who brought this script to East Anglia may have come from southern Denmark. A scatter of more recent finds suggests that others of the earliest runic monuments of England have Scandinavian affinities.

The pre-Christian inscriptions of Anglo-Saxon England are restricted to a few areas mainly in the south and east of the country: Kent and the Isle of Wight/Sussex, East Anglia and the East Midlands. They are all on portable objects and are short, often badly preserved, and almost always uncertain of meaning. Two or three examples will serve as illustration. On the seashore at Selsey, Sussex, were picked up two small strips of gold, which look as if they came from the same object, whatever it may have been. They are broken off at the ends, and corrugated into zigzags of five or six elements. Each piece has runes scratched on it. One reads 'b r n r n', which does not look as if it ever meant anything. The other reads 'a n m æ', too short and incomplete to interpret.

A plate fitted to the back of the mouthpiece of a scabbard buried in a sixth-century grave at Chessell Down, Isle of Wight, has a set of seven runes, divided by two dashes in vertical line into groups of three and four. The first letter of the second group is ᛉ, which, as has been seen, could be the variant *s*-rune, though if it is that it is the earliest example known. The text then reads 'æ c o: s œ r i', but its meaning has so far escaped runologists, despite a century or so of efforts. The runes would have been on the back of the scabbard, and so invisible when it was in use; and they are probably a later addition, cut shortly before the sword was buried, which suggests curious speculations about the purpose of the inscription.

Again, there are runes cut before firing in the clay of a ? sixth-century cremation urn excavated in the cemetery of Loveden Hill, Lincolnshire. But what on earth is a writer likely to have cut on a cremation urn? The runes are roughly formed, and not all characters are clearly readable, but it seems to say, 'sⁱþ æ b æ d‖þ i c w‖h l æ (.)', with pairs of vertical strokes dividing the text into words. The first group could be a personal name, presumably that of the man in the pot, but again the rest is baffling.

There are some fifteen inscriptions that can confidently be dated to this pre-Christian period, that is before 650 AD, on sword-pommels, a bracteate, brooches, a bronze bowl imported from the eastern Mediterranean (where the runes cut across the original stamped decorative frieze of hunting animals), and other portable objects. At this stage dating is entirely on archaeological grounds, and it must inevitably be somewhat speculative and insecure. Firm dating and certain interpretation does not begin until the Anglo-Saxons began to strike coins and by then they were also aware of the Roman alphabet. The earliest Anglo-Saxon coins were of gold, and manufactured in the first

Runes cut before firing in the clay of a cremation urn from the cemetery at Loveden Hill, Lincolnshire.

Fig. 8 Coins of
the moneyer Pada.

half of the seventh century. There was a fairly rapid devaluation, running through pale
gold (that is, gold alloyed with silver) to silver itself, which remained the common metal
for currency for many centuries. Some early coins had Roman superscriptions, imitating
their Roman or Merovingian prototypes, but there were also runic issues. The first runic
issue of any size was that of a moneyer called Pada, who copied fourth-century Roman
coins and put his name, 'p a d a', on the reverse. Towards the end of the seventh century
there was a silver coinage, the so-called *sceattas*, inscribed with the moneyer's name *Epa*,
variously spelled 'e p a', 'æ p a'; this was so popular that it was copied widely, even on
the mainland of the Low Countries. Other moneyers of this period who use runes were
Wigræd and Tilberht.

The mid-eighth century sees the appearance of an important runic coinage of some
sophistication. Now it is a royal issue, the weight and quality of the metal guaranteed by
the king's name and title on each piece. The obverse names Beonna, king of East Anglia
c. 750 AD, and the reverse has the moneyer's name. Three moneyers are known, Efe, who
uses Roman script for his name, and Wilred and Werferth, who employ runes. The king's
name and title is sometimes in runes, in the form 'b e o n n a r e x', but sometimes in
Roman or in a mixture of the scripts.

Coins are comparatively plentiful, and numismatists can ascribe them to particular
centuries and regions with some precision. In consequence they are important in
showing the spread of runic usage, from the south-east and east of England to the
Midlands, where the great King Offa of Mercia issued a rich coinage, with many runic
coins minted probably in East Anglia. Thence runes spread to the north, where runic
coins of the type called *stycas* continued in use in the ninth century. This shift, from a
preponderance of runic inscriptions in the south to one in the north and north Midlands,
is a significant one for the development of the runic script in England. The most important innovation of the Christian period was the appearance of runic memorial stones.
These are found almost exclusively in northern and north Midland areas (and that
includes parts of lowland Scotland in the Anglo-Saxon period). To those who think
runes were a script with magical and pagan links, it will come as a surprise to learn that
the Christian church not only encouraged their use but helped to extend their useful life
in England. Sometimes runes were used side by side with Roman script, sometimes
intermingled with it, sometimes instead of it.

The texts of the Anglo-Saxon rune-stones – as usual with Anglo-Saxon inscriptions –
are not very exciting in content, but they present important records of the different local
dialects, since their geographical distribution is clear and they can often be dated on the
basis of their sculptural decoration. We assume that a rune-stone records the dialect of
the region where it was found in modern times, since it is fairly unlikely that a sculptured
stone would be moved from one place to another in the early Middle Ages – different in
this respect from a sword, brooch or ring which could be passed from hand to hand and
district to district.

Fig. 9 The Anglo-Saxon runic inscriptions.

The simplest type of memorial inscription gives only the name of the deceased, like 'ti d f i r þ' on a stone from Monkwearmouth, Tyne and Wear, or, with an initial cross, '+ j i s l h e a r d' on a grave-slab at Dover, one of the few southern examples. In some grave-markers from Lindisfarne, Northumberland, there are separate texts in runes and Roman, and in at least one case the two texts record the same name. From Hartlepool is a group of similar grave-stones, each of which has an incised cross and a name, either in runes or Roman script. Very elegant and beautifully preserved is one with *alpha* and *omega* in the top quadrants formed by the cross, and the name 'h i l d i þ r y þ' divided in two in the lower quadrants. The runes are carefully cut and have neat serifs, which suggests that the mason who cut them was trained in Roman script too.

A Christian memorial stone from Monkwearmouth, Tyne and Wear, commemorating one Tidfirth.

The elegantly carved grave-slab of Hildithryth, found in an Anglo-Saxon cemetery at Hartlepool.

More elaborate is the text which gives the name of the deceased, but also that of the person who put up the monument. An example is a standing stone at Thornhill, West Yorkshire, with a sculptured interlace panel and below it three lines of runes: '+ e a d r e d | s e t e æ f t e | e a t e i n n e', 'Eadred set (this stone) in memory of Eadthegn'. A more elaborate version of this type of epitaph is on another Thornhill stone with a more elaborate interlace, a pricier memorial altogether. The text reads '+ j i l s u i þ : a r æ r d e : æ f t (.) | b e r h t s u i þ e . b e k u n | o n b e r g i g e b i d d a þ | þ æ r : s a u l e', '+Gilswith raised up a memorial [*bekun* = modern English *beacon*] on a mound in memory of Berhtswith. Pray for (her) soul'. Both names here are of women. Similar is an inscription on a shaft at Great Urswick, Cumbria: '+ t u n w i n i s e t æ | æ f t e r t o r o i | t r e d æ b e k u | n æ f t e r h i s b | æ u r n æ g e b i d æ s þ e | r s | a u | l æ', '+ Tunwini set in memory of Torh-tred a memorial in memory of his ?child. Pray for his soul.' The runes are crudely cut and badly set out, while the rest of the sculptured work on the monument is very second-rate. Despite this, the craftsman was proud enough of his work to want to sign it, so he carved his signature across the lower part of the stone face. 'l y l þ i s w-' remains, but the end of the text was hacked away when the shaft was re-used as building material: *Lyl þis w(orhtæ)*, 'Lyl made this.'

By comparing these examples, you can see some of the dialectal or chronological features of Old English that such monuments attest. The verb 'set' is *setæ* on Great Urswick, *sete* on the first Thornhill stone. Great Urswick represents the earlier pronunciation of the verbal ending, Thornhill the later. The imperative 'pray' is *gebidæs* on Great Urswick, *gebiddaþ* on the second Thornhill stone. Thornhill presents the more formal verbal ending, Great Urswick perhaps a local dialectal variant or a demotic form.

There is a further point of interest in some of these examples. Just as, in modern times, epitaphs and *In Memoriam* announcements in newspapers sometimes include short

38

The re-used cross-shaft at Great Urswick, Cumbria, with the memorial inscription above and the maker's signature cut untidily across the two lower figures.

passages of verse, so do these Anglo-Saxon epitaphs. Anglo-Saxon verse is different from more recent English verse. It seldom rhymes, but instead requires alliteration within a line. So, set out in a formal editorial manner, the two longer epitaphs quoted would run:

Tunwini setæ   æfter Torohtredæ
bekun æfter his bæurnæ.   Gebidæs þer saulæ.

and:

Jilsuiþ aræde   æft(.) Berhtsuiþe
bekun on bergi.   Gebiddaþ þær saule.

The most important verse inscription on an Anglo-Saxon rune-stone is not, however, memorial. It occurs on the superb eighth-century cross in the church at Ruthwell, Dumfries and Galloway, one of the greatest pieces of stone sculpture from early times in the United Kingdom. The north and south faces of this cross have panels depicting incidents in the life (and death) of Christ and of the Fathers. East and west faces have plant scrolls with birds and beasts, and in the margins a series of lines of runes, set two, three or four to the line. They reproduce part of an early version of a poem on the cross which is also known in a later, written, text, usually called *The Dream of the Rood*. The Ruthwell cross was severely battered in the religious storms of seventeenth-century Scotland, so some of the text has been destroyed. What remains is in remarkably good condition, suggesting that the monument spent most of its history indoors and protected from the weather. The surviving section of the poem, supplemented by a few bits of material from other sources, is:

(+Ond)geredæ hinæ God almeittig
þa he walde on galgu gistiga
modig fore (.) men ...
(Ahof) ic riicnæ kyninc
heafunæs hlafard. Hælda ic ni dorstæ.
Bismærædu unket men ba ætgadre.
Ic (wæs) miþ blodæ bistemid ...
+Krist wæs on rodi.
Hweþræ þer fusæ fearran kwomu
æþþilæ til anum. Ic þæt al biheald.
Sare ic wæs miþ sorgum gidrœfid.
Hnag.....
miþ strelum giwundad.
Alegdun hiæ hinæ limwœrignæ.
Gistoddun him (æt his) licæs heafdum.
Bihealdu hiæ þer ...

'Almighty God stripped himself as he prepared to climb the gallows, valiant in men's sight ... I raised up a great king, lord of heaven. I dared not bow down. Men reviled us both together. I was drenched with blood ... Christ was on the cross. Yet to him in his solitude came noble men, eager, from afar. I beheld it all. I was bitterly troubled with griefs. I bowed ... wounded with arrows. Down they laid that limb-weary one. They stood at the corpse's head. There they beheld ...'

The scramasax with its inlaid *futhork* and the man's name Beagnoth, recovered from the River Thames at Battersea.

The later period also saw runes used on portable objects, in both the north and south of England. Not surprisingly, the content of these inscriptions varies a good deal. Important is a scramasax (a short sword with a single-edged blade) found in the Thames near Battersea in the nineteenth century; important because it provides the only epigraphical *futhork*. It is a prestige weapon, dated by archaeologists to the late ninth century. In the blade the smith cut patterned grooves, and inlaid them with different metals, copper, bronze and silver. The effect is a rich one of coloured decorative lines, but the smith did not restrict himself to decoration. He also engraved and inlaid a *futhork* of twenty-eight runes, some of them of unusual form, perhaps variant and perhaps erroneous. And he added the personal name 'b e a g n o þ', presumably either his own or that of the weapon's owner.

Three runic boxes were discovered outside England, though how and when they got to their find-places can only be conjecture. In the Herzog Anton Ulrich-Museum, Brunswick, is an elaborately carved ivory box from the eighth century. It may have come from the church treasury at nearby Gandersheim. A metal plate is affixed to its base and on it are carved elegant runes, carefully set out. They form two texts, or rather one repeated. Unfortunately nobody has produced a convincing interpretation. In the church at Mortain, Normandy, is a small beech-wood box in the general form of a house. Copper-gilt plates cover the wood, and these are adorned with repoussé decoration with representations of Christ and angels. Impressed into the roof of the box are three uneven lines of runes: '+ g o o d h e l p e : æ a d a n þ i i o s n e c i i s m e e l g e w a r a h t æ', 'God help Æada (who) made this ?reliquary'. The text is in the northern or north Midland dialect of Old English.

Most famous of the English runic objects is probably the Franks Casket, named after Sir Augustus Wollaston Franks through whom it (or rather, most of it) came to the British Museum. This is a whalebone box, first known in the nineteenth century in the possession of a farmer at Auzon, Haute-Loire, France, whose family used it as a work box. The farmer's son removed the silver fittings covering the pegs that held the sides and corner-posts together, and the box fell, or more probably was ripped, apart. Three sides, top and base came to Franks who gave them to the British Museum. The fourth side turned up later, was separately acquired by a collector and ended up in the Bargello Museum, Florence, though the British Museum has a cast of it. All sides and the top panel are richly carved and have inscriptions, which attest a dialect from northern or north Midland England.

All the inscriptions save the main one on the front are related to the sculptured panels they stand in or next to. For instance, on the top is a scene showing an archer defending a stockade against armed enemies. Above him is his name, 'æ g i l i'. On the front is a scene showing the Adoration of Christ: in a small panel above is the title 'm æ g i', 'Magi'.

The carved panel on the top of the Franks Casket, with its scene of the archer Ægili defending his house against armed raiders.

One side depicts the wolf suckling Romulus and Remus, and the inscription runs round the picture: 'romwalus and reumwalus twœgen gibroþær afœddæ hiæ wylif in romæcæstri: oþlæ unneg', 'Romulus and Remus, two brothers, a she-wolf nourished them in Rome, far from their native land'.

The back depicts the Emperor Titus's capture of Jerusalem, with the temple at the centre, attackers to the left and fugitives to the right. The descriptive text is partly in runes, partly in Roman, partly in Old English, partly in Latin. It begins 'her fegtaþ titus end giuþeasu', probably 'Here fight Titus and the Jews', though the form of the last word is odd. Then it continues in a mixture of Roman characters HIC FUGIANT HIERUSALIM, the sentence continued in runic 'afitatores'. The Latin is neither perfect nor classical, and should be *hic fugiunt Hierusalim habitatores*, 'Here the inhabitants flee from Jerusalem'. Two smaller scenes at the bottom of the panel have their own short titles, 'd o m', 'judgment, court', and 'g i s l', 'hostage'.

The right side is problematic. The scene it represents is complex and mysterious; it has not yet been satisfactorily identified, and may never be since we may have lost the story it illustrates. The inscription is partly in code, for instead of the usual vowel runes, the carver uses forms of his own invention, deliberately to obscure the meaning. Though the code has been cracked, the meaning of the verse inscription remains obscure.

Finally, the main inscription on the front of the casket. This is the only one that does not refer to any carved scene on the box; instead it gives a riddling explanation of where the material for making it came from. In verse form:

> fisc.flodu ahof on fergenberig.
> warþ gasric grorn þær he on greut giswom.

There are grammatical difficulties in the text that make exact translation hard, but a reasonable attempt is: 'the fish beat up the seas on to the mountainous cliff; the king of terror became sad when he swam on to the shingle'. The final bit of the text gives the answer to the riddle, 'h r o n æ s b a n', 'whale's bone'. In other words, the box was made from the bone of a beached whale.

Some of the later inscriptions come from known ecclesiastical contexts, and these suggest a reading audience of a learned or semi-literate sort. We have seen that a Hartlepool grave marker has seriffed runes in 'h i l d i þ r y þ', together with *alpha* and *omega*, and it is most likely that such a stone came from the cemetery of the Anglo-Saxon monastery there. From a habitation site at Brandon, Suffolk, comes a pair of tweezers with the personal name '+ a l d r e d' also in neat seriffed letters, and excavators have suggested that this site too may be ecclesiastical. Part of a bone comb was picked up from a rubbish dump at Whitby, again probably from the local monastery. Its text begins in Latin and continues in Old English: 'd(æ) u s mæ u s g o d a l u w a l u d o h e l i p æ c y-', 'My God: God almighty help Cyn-', with the rest of the ?owner's name broken away.

Most important is an object that can be dated precisely. This is the coffin made by the monks of Lindisfarne for the body of St Cuthbert in 698, and now in Durham. Incised figures, of Christ and Mary, apostles, archangels and evangelists, cover its lid and sides. It seems that all the figures had their names cut in to identify them, faintly and with a knife point. They are very hard to make out now, and were probably never very distinct, so who was expected to read them is anybody's guess. Most names were in Roman, but the Christ symbol, 'i h s x p s' is runic, and so are the evangelist names Matthew, Mark and John, though Luke is in Roman.

Clearly many of the later inscriptions show that runes were not the only letters the carver (or designer) knew. The occasional use of Latin in an inscription shows a learned society in which Roman script would be common. Some pieces show Roman and runic used for different purposes. For instance, though the Ruthwell cross is famous for its runic verse text in Old English, it also has Latin explanations of its carvings in Roman script. There are cases of a single text mixing runic and Roman letters. A memorial stone at Chester-le-Street has the name *Eadmund* cut in two lines: only 'm' and 'n' are runes, the rest Roman. A finger-ring found at Llysfaen, Clwyd, has the ?owner's name, +ALHSTAn, with only the last letter runic. This sort of mixture is common enough on the later coinage. A ninth-century gold finger-ring from Lancashire, probably Manchester, has the mixed legend: + æDRED MEC AH EAnRED MEC agROf, 'Ædred owns me, Eanred engraved me.'

There was certainly some sort of rivalry between the scripts in the later Anglo-Saxon period. It was not, as some have suggested, a religious rivalry or conflict. There is no reason at all to think that the Christian church disapproved of the pagan script, runes. Quite the contrary, since Christians used runes on the coffin of a great saint and on their memorial stones, and the assertively Christian Ruthwell sculptures were amplified with a Christian poem inscribed in runes. Yet the old script inevitably fought a losing battle against the more prestigious Roman, and ultimately could not survive the competition. The later monuments I have described here are mainly from the seventh, eighth and ninth centuries. Thereafter Anglo-Saxon runes are hard to find, and it is unlikely the script survived the Norman Conquest.

A gold ring with a mixed legend of runes and Roman letters from Lancashire, probably Manchester.

5
Runes and the Vikings

The Norse inscriptions in the younger *futhark* form the most important epigraphical archive of any Germanic people. The time during which the new runes were being developed – say, *c.* 700 AD – was also a time of significant change in the Scandinavian languages and, from then on right into the later Middle Ages, language change is traceable in a succession of inscribed objects, often dateable on the grounds of history, archaeology or art history. One must, of course, remember that spelling change lags a good deal behind change in pronunciation as the chaotic spelling of modern English reveals, while the small number of characters in the younger *futhark* makes it inefficient as a spelling apparatus.

More generally interesting, however, is the contribution of the runic inscriptions to our knowledge of Norse history. The period of use of the younger *futhark* coincided to a good extent with the Age of the Vikings (*c.* 800–1100 AD). Inevitably the inscriptions reflect the views and actions of that time, though they have a bias of distribution towards the later part of the period and towards parts of Sweden rather than Norway and Denmark. Most contemporary accounts of the Vikings were written by their enemies, by the Franks, the English, the Irish and other peoples they preyed upon. Not surprisingly they are unsympathetic to the Norsemen, reporting them as pirates, raiders, merciless killers, treacherous enemies, pillagers of the Church and so on. Certainly they were all these, but there were other sides to Viking activity which were neglected by those who saw them only as wolves of slaughter.

The inscriptions tell us something of the Vikings' side of things. Much of the material is on the great rune-stones that were so characteristic of the age. The rune-stones are often memorials, commemorating the great dead and frequently those who died far from their home lands. But not always. Some Vikings put up stones in their own honour, *eftir sik siálfan*, 'in honour of the man himself', or *at sik kvikvan*, 'in his own lifetime', to boast of deeds that they thought praiseworthy. And some were put up in sheer self-glory, as acts of propaganda.

Most rune-stones were free-standing, often natural boulders. Occasionally a rune-master would cut an inscription on the face of a living rock, preferably one that could be seen at a distance, or was by a strategic road or river crossing. The carving might consist only of the inscription, with the runes cut in successive lines between incised frames, or the stone might have considerable decoration, and the runes be cut on part of the pattern, often along the body of a serpentine monster. In many, perhaps most, cases the letters would be coloured in, though little of this paintwork remains today. (Some Scandinavian countries persist in the pernicious practice of repainting in the letters, which of course makes it hard to see with certainty the original incisions.) Occasionally there is an expensive rune-stone with all its faces covered with decoration.

The most famous example of this is the great stone at Jelling, a small market town in Jylland, Denmark. Here the stone forms only part of a group of monuments in which a

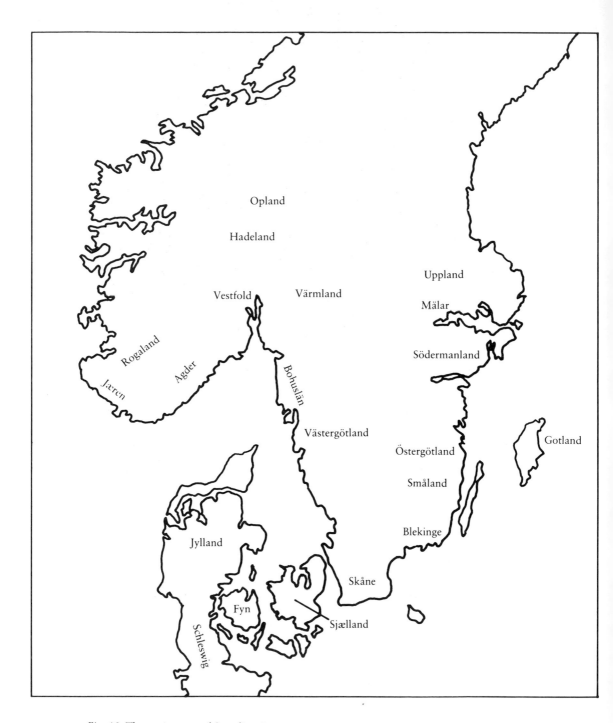

Fig. 10 The runic areas of Scandinavia.

The main inscription of Haraldr Bluetooth's great memorial stone to his parents at Jelling, Jylland.

pair of kings, father and son, publicly displayed their grandeur. Prominent in the complex are two mounds, to the north and south of the later Romanesque church. The northern mound once contained a pagan burial in a wooden chamber. The southern one was always empty. Midway between the mound centres (and just outside the church) are two rune-stones, one of which may have been moved here from another site nearby. The smaller stone is the simpler and earlier. It has no ornament; simply the text:

:kurmR:kunukR:	King Gormr
:karþi:kubl:þusi:	made this monument
:aft:þurui:kunu	in memory of his wife Thorvi,
:sina:tanmarkaR:but:	Denmark's adornment.

The greater stone – it is nearly two and a half metres high – is an irregular granite boulder whose shape gives it three main faces. Two have low relief carving, of a crucified Christ and a monstrous raging beast. Most of the text is on the third side, in four lines, but there is a further line along the bottom of each of the carved sides. The whole text reads:

:haraltr:kunukR:baþ:kaurua
kubl:þausi:aft:kurmfaþursin
aukaft:þaurui:muþur:sina:sa
haraltr:ias:saR·uan·tanmaurk
:ala·auknuruiak
auktanikarþi kristna

'King Haraldr ordered this monument to be made in memory of his father Gormr and his mother Thorvi. This was the Haraldr who won all Denmark for himself and Norway, and made the Danes Christian.' These characters are known from other sources, so the stone can be dated with fair precision. Gormr does not appear in contemporary records but the eleventh-century historian Adam of Bremen describes him as an opponent of the Christian mission to Denmark a century or so earlier. Better known is Haraldr, nicknamed Bluetooth. He became Christian *c*. 960 AD and died in the 980s. He seems to have exercised some overlordship over the great Earl Hákon of Norway, and this may account for the claim that he won Norway. His assertion that he 'won all Denmark for himself' is a baffling one since we know little about internal Danish politics at the time. It may mean that he re-unified the land or brought outlying provinces firmly under control. Beneath the Romanesque church at Jelling archaeologists found traces of earlier timber churches, and the earliest was probably Haraldr's. In it there seems to have been a major burial, and it is possible that Haraldr, on his conversion, removed his pagan father's body from the north mound and gave it decent Christian burial, at the same time adding his own, empty, mound to the south to improve the magnificent effect.

This was a royal family, and few Vikings could afford, or need, such an arrogant display. Lower down the social scale is a member of the landed aristocracy, one Jarlabanki who lived at Täby, Uppland, Sweden, in the eleventh century. He owned the manor there and carried out road improvements, thinking it worth a bit of self-advertisement. He constructed a causeway (*brú*, 'bridge') and recorded his enterprise on four rune-stones which stood, and still stand, two at each end. They say, 'Jarlabanki had this stone put up in his own lifetime. And he made this causeway for his soul's sake. And he owned the whole of Täby by himself. May God help his soul.' At nearby Vallentuna he put up another stone which repeats the content of the Täby ones and adds: 'and he made this meeting-place, and he alone held this district.' These are not Jarlabanki's only monument. His son Ingifastr put up a stone to commemorate his father, and indeed the family is quite well known in rune-stones in the district.

Less ambitious again, or at any rate less self-important, was Áli, also from Uppland, who put up a single stone to glorify himself. 'Áli had this stone put up in his own honour. He took Knútr's *danegeld* in England. May God help his soul.' This presents a new perspective. Whereas the stones quoted hitherto have glorified leaders for their local importance, this is the stone of a real Viking, one who left his homeland for adventure or profit abroad, and presumably brought back his winnings to invest in land or stock. It also gives a fascinating bit of historical fact. Knútr (Cnut, perhaps better known to English readers as Canute) was a Danish prince, and we might think that the armies he led to England in the early eleventh century were raised from the Danes. Yet here is a man from the heartland of Sweden who served with him and got his reward. Runic evidence then shows that Norwegians too joined Knútr's armies. At Galteland, Aust-Agder, Norway, was found a stone put up by one Arnsteinn in memory of his son Biórr: 'He was killed in the guard when Knútr attacked England.'

Rune-stones commemorating the dead are more common than those put up by the living to themselves. A good repute after death was important to Norse belief, and the rune-stones were one way of ensuring this. Yet there may have been another reason for putting up such stones. It was important to publish a man's death, particularly if he was of the property-owning class and had met his end away from home. Someone had to claim the estate; the rune-stone, proclaiming a death to the world, could be the authority. This may be why so many rune-stones are in public places, at meeting-fields, by main road sides and so on. They are public documents, like death announcements in newspapers. The rune-stones may record circumstances of death, place of burial, major events in the life of the dead man, relationship to the living, ownership of an estate, etc. In so doing they record the pattern of the Viking Age, at any rate as some – apparently the better-off – Vikings saw it.

Recent scholars have played down the 'battle, murder and sudden death' aspects of Viking life, preferring to stress their importance as merchants, colonists and explorers. The rune-stones are not so mealy-mouthed. They often boast of a dead Viking's murderous exploits. Sometimes these were in Scandinavia itself. There are a couple of rune-stones in Skåne that refer to a battle at Upsala. That at Hällestad was erected by one Áskell to his gracious lord Tóki Gormsson. After this statement it breaks into verse:

> He fled not at Upsala.
> Comrades set up after their brother
> A stone on the hill, steadied with runes.
> They kept closest to Gormr's Tóki.

A memorial stone from Hällestad, Skåne, with a verse inscription recording the valour of Tóki Gormsson, killed in battle at Upsala.

At Västra Strö, also in Skåne, is a stone which forms part of a grave monument, made by a man for his brother. 'He met his death in the north, *í víkingu*, in a Viking exploit'. On a memorial at Tirsted, Lolland, Denmark, is an elaborate, though dyslexic, epitaph to one Fraþi: 'He was then the *fqink* [? = terror] of men, and he met his death in Sweden, and was ?the foremost of Frekki's guard: all Vikings.'

Yet adventures abroad are more evocative of Viking activity. Many are mentioned on rune-stones, though curiously enough they say practically nothing about one that seems to us most exciting – the perilous journey of exploration west over the Atlantic to Greenland and America. We have seen a Swede and a Norwegian a-Vikinging in England, and there were of course Danes too, like Manni and Sveinn, commemorated on a stone at Valleberga, Skåne, who *liggia í Lundúnum*, 'are buried in London.' Other countries too the western Vikings attacked or worked in. According to a stone at Djulefors, Södermanland, Sweden, a man Óláfr 'ploughed the seas in the east and died in Lombardy.' Guðvér, whom his sons called their 'bold father', shared *danegeld* in England and *borgir á Saxlandi sótti karla*, 'like a man attacked cities in Saxland [probably Germany]' (Grinda, Södermanland). Stones are not the only runic records of Viking enterprise in the west. On a silver neck-ring which made up part of a small Viking hoard found at Senja, Troms, Norway, is a verse couplet which, I suppose, accounted for where the silver came from:

> *Fórum drengja Fríslands á vit,*   We went to visit the young lads of Frisia,
> *ok vígs fǫtum vér skiptum*   and we it was who split the spoils of war.

More frequently mentioned are the exploits in the East, the men who followed the dangerous but profitable route across the Baltic, through Russia to the Eastern Roman Empire (which the Vikings called *Grikkland*, 'Greece') and Arab territory. Many Vikings, particularly from Uppland and the Baltic island of Gotland, made their money there, trading, levying tribute, raiding or a mixture of all three. For instance, a stone at Ulunda, Uppland, tells of a Viking who 'journeyed boldly and made money among the Greeks for his heir' – note the stress on inheritance. At Veda, also in Uppland, is an epitaph to Irenmundr who 'bought this estate and made his money in the East, in *Garðar* [this name means 'the cities', is cognate with the Russian element *-grad, -gorod*, and is used by the Vikings as a general designation for the Russian trading towns]'. This is how a Viking invested his spoils.

Inscriptions trace the voyages over the Baltic, as that of Mervalla, set up for Sveinn, a ship's captain, who 'often sailed in his fine freighter to Semigallen round Domesnäs [C. Kolkas on the northern tip of Latvia].' To Estonia where Bjǫrn 'fell in Viromaa' (Ängby, Uppland). To Livonia where Bergvið drowned (Åda, Södermanland). Down the rivers into Russia and the great trading station of Novgorod, which the Vikings called *Holmgarðr*. Somewhere on the way, 'between Vitaholm and Garðar', Thóraldr died (Alstad, Opland, Norway), and an unknown sailor – his name has been lost from the stone – drowned in the lake near Holmgarðr when 'his cargo-ship went down: only three escaped with their lives'. At Sjusta, Uppland, a rock inscription tells of Spiallbuþi who 'died in Novgorod in the church of (St) Óláfr'. That there should be a church in a Russian town dedicated to the royal saint of Norway suggests a permanent Scandinavian colony there. At Turinge, Södermanland, lived a man called Thorsteinn. When he died abroad his family and friends put up an impressive monument with a verse inscription. This describes him as one of a pair of brothers who were 'the best of men, both at home and out on active service'. His visit to Russia was not for peaceful trading.

> He died in battle, east in Russia,
> Leader of the guard, best of landsmen.

South of Novgorod the trade route followed the Dnieper, past Kiev to the Black Sea and the heart of the Eastern Empire, with Byzantium as the goal. Not all Vikings came to this great capital to buy and sell. A promising occupation for a young tough was to become a member of the Varangian Guard of the Emperor. At Ed, Uppland, a man called Rǫgnvaldr had a boulder inscribed to his mother's memory. He says little about her, but boasts of his own position. In the Eastern Empire (*á Grikklandi*, 'in Greece') he was *liðs foringi*, 'captain of the guard'. But there was trading too. A ship's captain called Liótr put up a stone at Fjuckby, Uppland, to his son's memory: he was called Áki and ventured abroad. 'He was master of a freighter, docking in the harbours of Greece. He died at home.'

The eastern route led also to *Serkland*, a land of dark-skinned (though not negroid) peoples, the Arab caliphates. Here too the Vikings penetrated, not always successfully. Notorious is an expedition mounted by a man Ingvarr, known in later fiction as Ingvarr the Far-travelled. Nearly thirty rune-stones in the Lake Mälar region of Sweden testify to the young men who embarked with Ingvarr and did not come back. It was a disaster of the early eleventh century, bringing down many youths of good family and adventurous disposition. Their purpose, and the appalling result, is defined by a stone at Gripsholm. 'Tóla had this stone set up in memory of her son Haraldr, Ingvarr's brother.' Then, in verse:

> Like men they went far to seek gold,
> And in the east they fed the eagle,
> Died in the south, in Serkland.

The image of feeding the eagle is a common one in early Norse literature, for everyone knows that eagles by preference eat the bodies of men killed in battle. Ingvarr's voyage was a heroic and bloody one, and his companions were professional killers looking for plunder. They got their come-uppance, as the sequence of mourning stones at home reveals. 'Thiálfi and Hólmlaug had all these stones set up in memory of Banki, their son. He was the sole owner of a ship. He sailed it east with Ingvarr's armada. May God help his soul.' 'Andvitr and Kiti and Kárr and Blesi and Diarfr put up this stone in memory of their father Gunnleifr. He fell in the east with Ingvarr. May God help his soul.' 'Spióti and Hálfdanr put up this stone in memory of their brother Skarþi. He went from here eastwards with Ingvarr. He lies in Serkland, Eyvindr's son.' And so on.

Of course the Viking Age, like most parts of the Middle Ages, was a time of bloodshed and short life. Instructive are two joint epitaphs. One, at Dalum, Västergötland, Sweden, is erected to two brothers: 'One died in the west, the other in the east.' Even more chilling is one of the texts on a stone at Högby, Östergötland, Sweden. 'Gulli, a man of good family, fathered five sons. Ásmundr, a valiant fighting-man, fell at Fyris [near Upsala and the site of a famous battle in the late tenth century]; Ǫzurr died in the east, among the Greeks; Hálfdanr was killed in Bornholm; Kári (?died. . . .); dead too is Búi.'

However, as the Jarlabanki stones show, not all inscriptions describe sudden death. Nor, as for that, were all voyages abroad necessarily for material profit. When Ástríðr of Broby, Uppland, commemorated her husband Eysteinn, she recorded that 'he visited Jerusalem and died among the Greeks'. It is likely he was on a pilgrimage. Christianity is quite strongly represented on the later stones, with pious hopes that God would help the deceased. Even a professional killer like Áli hoped for God's grace while boasting that he had taken *danegeld* in Knútr's army. Sometimes the Christianity goes farther than this, informing the man's behaviour through life. This was the case of ?Eyvindr whose son remembered his virtues on a stone at Rörbro, Småland, Sweden. The verse epitaph says he was incapable of shameful action (*mestr úníðingr*), he begrudged no food (to his dependants, to the poor) and he loathed strife. It ends: 'A good man, he held the faith of the good God.' In contrast, some stones that date from the late years of the pagan period have invocations to the god Thor, perhaps in answer to the challenge of Christianity. So, a stone at Virring, Jylland, ends its text, **Þórr vígi þessi kuml**, 'Thor hallow this monument'. Alternatively there is the formula 'Thor hallow these runes'.

Jarlabanki's bridge-building was an act of social charity as well as self-advertisement, and there are several other examples of the same thing. A stone at Sälna, Uppland, names three brothers who put it up and built a bridge in their father's memory. 'God help his spirit and soul and forgive him his trespasses and sins.' Then the inscription breaks into verse:

Always will it stand
while time lives on,
this bridge firmly founded
broad in memory of a good man.
Lads made it
for their father.
No way-monument can be
better made.

There are other social acts recorded on these memorials: building a *sæluhús*, a hostel for wayfarers in the wild, or establishing a thing-place, an open-air meeting place where the community could hold its court. Such a thing-place would be designated by standing marker stones, and among these could be the rune-stone recording the founder's family and possessions. It is perhaps this link with legal meetings that explains the strong element of pride in place and inheritance that some rune-stones show. Probably the most detailed example is at Hillersjö, Uppland, though here the inscription is on a rock-face where any passer-by could take note of the changing pattern of ownership. 'Geirmundr married Geirlaug when she was a virgin. They had a son before he [= Geirmundr] drowned. Then the son died. Then she married Guðríkr. He [... about 25 runes missing]. Then they had children, but only one daughter lived. She was called Inga. Ragnfastr of Snottsta married her. Then he died and a son afterwards. And the mother [= Inga] took inheritance after her son. Then she married Eiríkr. Then she died. At that Geirlaug took inheritance after her daughter Inga.' It was a complicated story and needed recording so that nobody could challenge a future right to hold property. Other stones in the neighbourhood mention this family and confirm the pattern of inheritance.

The Hillersjö text opens with an exhortation to the passer-by to take note of the history: 'Read the runes!'

Other stones have similar genealogical material, accompanied by statements of inheritance. But the family was not the only institution that bonded Viking society together, and rune-stones sometimes define other relationships. Some refer to a man as another's *félagi*. This word was borrowed into English where it became 'fellow'. Its primary meaning is shown by its etymology. The first element is Old Norse *fé*, 'money'; the second is related to the verb *leggia*, 'to lay'. Thus a 'fellow' is someone who laid down money in a common enterprise, a business partner. This sense is certainly recorded in runes. A notable example is on a Viking stone outside Scandinavia. On the island of Berezan' at the mouth of the Dnieper in southern Russia was found a stone with a damaged inscription which probably read 'Brandr made this stone coffin for his partner Karl'. Presumably this is a relic of two partners in trade, one of whom died on their travels. The other, taking over the joint business (and holding responsibility to Karl's heirs for his share of the investment) used this gravestone to declare his legal position.

This meaning may be evidenced on a stone at Århus, Jylland, which three men devised in memory of a fourth, Qzurr Saxi, their *félagi*. He and a man Árni owned a ship in common, and the group may have formed a partnership. There is, however, an extended meaning of *félagi* that appears on rune-stones, and this may be a case of it. It seems sometimes to refer to a member of a closed group, such as a force of armed men, and then probably means 'comrade, comrade-in-arms'. On this Århus stone Qzurr is also described as a very good *drengr*, a word which in these contexts is to be translated 'young fighting-man'. The title is quite common on these memorials though the military connotation is not always clear. A good example is on a stone at Haddeby, Schleswig. This was raised by Thórólfr, described as Sveinn's *hempægi*, and commemorates his *félagi*, Eiríkr, 'who met his death when *drengiar* (plural of *drengr*) besieged Haddeby. He was master of a ship, and a very good *drengr*.' Clearly Thórólfr and Eiríkr belonged to the same unit. They were fellows, *drengiar*, and Thórólfr has a further title: he is *hempægi* of a certain Sveinn. This title, *hempægi*, means literally 'home-receiver', and refers to a member of a noble's household, his retainer. Sveinn was apparently a king, since another Haddeby stone refers to the same siege: 'King Sveinn set this stone in memory of Skarði his *hempægi*, who had travelled in the west and has now met his death at Haddeby.' A further title on rune-stones is *þegn*, literally 'servant' but here a servant of high grade, an official, an older man who was officer to a king or a nobleman. There are also occasional references to titles of rank, of which *landmannr*, literally 'landsman', is one. And there are occasional specific and responsible positions: one is that of *víkingavǫrðr*, the man who had the duty of co-ordinating defence against pirates.

In this later Viking Age we get the impression of a coherent and ordered society, hierarchical and with clearly defined ranks below that of king. In this society women had their proper place. They could, as we have seen, inherit and control property. They often took the initiative in raising rune-stones, and since their husbands often died far from home they must have had great responsibility for keeping a household intact and thriving. Yet it is comparatively rare to find rune-stones raised in their memory. A famous example is the graceful and elegantly decorated pillar from Dynna, Opland, Norway, which once stood on a grave-mound at the farm there. With its incised

52

decoration of the Three Wise Men under the
Christmas star, this is a work from the early
Christian period, and the inscription describes one of those acts of social and
Christian charity we have seen earlier: *Gunnvǫr gerði brú, Þrýðríks dóttir, eftir Ástríði,
dóttur sína. Sú var mær hǫnnurst á Haðal-
andi*, 'Gunnvǫr, Thrýðrík's daughter, made
a bridge in memory of her daughter Ástríðr.
She was the most skilful girl in Hadeland.'
No bad epitaph to take with you through
eternity.

The monument to Ástríðr,
'most skilful girl in Hadeland',
from Dynna, Opland.

6
Scandinavian Runes
in the British Isles

The Vikings were a far-travelled people, and they took their runes with them. It is odd, however, that Norse runes do not always turn up where you expect them. None are known from Normandy, although that was settled by Scandinavians. From the ninth century onwards Iceland was occupied by people largely of Norwegian stock, but surviving runes there are late and of the post-Viking Age. Few runes have been found in the Faroe Islands, again a Scandinavian possession. Though rune-stones make it clear that Vikings were very active in Russia and the East, yet again only a handful of runic monuments remain there, though these include such exotic items as the name *Hálfdanr* scratched on the marble of the great church of Hagia Sophia, Istanbul, and an inscription, hardly readable these days, cut on a marble lion once at Piraeus and now outside the Arsenal, Venice.

The Vikings certainly brought runes with them to the British Isles, but there are nowhere near as many monuments here as we might expect, and their geographical distribution is curious. In the ninth and tenth centuries large parts of northern and eastern England were under the control of Scandinavian incomers. In the tenth century a Norwegian king ruled in York, and in the early eleventh there were Danish kings on the English throne. Yet Viking runic finds are rare in England. In Ireland there was a strong if intermittent Viking presence for a couple of centuries; again, runic finds are few, and were even fewer before recent excavations delved into the Norse layers of Dublin. In contrast stands the tiny Isle of Man, midway between. Here the Scandinavian settlers used runes freely in the tenth and eleventh centuries, and their memorial crosses remain as evidence. Orkney and Shetland were Norwegian territory in the Viking Age and for centuries afterwards. There is a scatter of Viking Age runes in each of the island groups and post-Viking Scandinavians were vigorous in cutting graffiti on the stones of the prehistoric burial chamber of Maeshowe in Orkney. Inscriptions are scattered through the Western Isles and the coastal mainland of Scotland, but they are surprisingly sparse considering the activity of the Vikings in those areas.

Why this should be I do not know. It may be that cutting runes and carving rune-stones in particular was the custom of a settled society, and that nomadic Vikings would not indulge in it. But this would not account for the dearth of inscriptions from the Danelaw or the Northern Isles after Viking occupation was established. Perhaps the social or commercial classes who were the prime users of runes were not represented among the Viking incomers to the British Isles. Or there may be local circumstances and influences that we know nothing about, for our detailed information on the history of some of these regions in Viking times is slight.

On the whole, the Norse runic monuments in England are an undistinguished lot. Outstanding, indeed splendid, is a carved slab that formed part of a grave monument in St Paul's churchyard, London. It is from the eleventh century, probably of Danish inspiration. The slab top has a magnificent beast carved in low relief and coloured dark blue with details picked out in brown and white. The edge of the stone has two lines of Danish runes: **k(i)na:let:lekia:st│in:þensi:auk:tuki:**, 'Ginna and Tóki had this stone laid.' Presumably there was once a matching slab saying whose grave it was. Winchester, capital of late Anglo-Saxon England, has also yielded a rune-stone, of which only a small fragment is preserved and that because it was built into the tower of a mediaeval church in the town. From the few letters that remain the text cannot be recovered, but an interesting aspect is that the runes retain traces of the red colouring that once distinguished them. The only other Danish runes in the south of England are casual graffiti, cut on animal bones from butcher's meat. They come from the eleventh-century levels at St Albans. Both are preserved only in part and one has the common text type *N risti rúnar*, 'N cut (these) runes', with the name incomplete. Also Danish, and perhaps an import, is a comb-case found at Lincoln. This is made up from pieces of bone, and cut along one of them is the advertising slogan, **kamb:koþan:kiari:þorfastr**, 'A good comb Thorfastr made.'

In the north of England Norse runes lasted a considerable time and were used in a bilingual community that mixed the Norse and English tongues. Unfortunately many of the monuments are fragmentary or weathered, and it is hard to establish textual details. Clear enough is a graffito on one of the stones of Carlisle cathedral (which cannot therefore be earlier than the late eleventh century). The text, in a mixture of Danish and short-twig runes, says: **tolfin:uraitþasirunraþisistain**, 'Dolfin wrote these runes on this stone.' Casual graffiti at Dearham, Cumbria, and Settle, N. Yorkshire, are only useful as giving geographical find-points. A sundial at Skelton-in-Cleveland had both Roman and runic texts, but only a few runes remain on the fragment that survives. At Pennington, Cumbria, is a tympanum stone, dated to the twelfth century, poorly preserved. The text seems to record the builder and mason of the church in a language that is bastard Norse, perhaps Norse-English. Finally, and most splendid, is a font at Bridekirk, Cumbria. The bowl is a square block elaborately carved on all four sides, and dated by art historians to the twelfth century. One side has a curling ribbon running between two capitals and surrounded by foliage. Below it sits a little figure, apparently with hammer and chisel, carving away. On the ribbon is an inscription recording the artist's name. The runes, mixed with a few bookhand characters, give a rhyming couplet in late Old or early Middle English:

+*Ricarþ he me iwrocte*	Richard he made me,
and to þis merð (?) me brocte	and ... brought me to this splendour.

In Ireland only three or four runic texts were known until recent years. There is one important rune-stone, in the cathedral at Killaloe, co. Clare. It has two inscriptions, one in runes and the Norse language, one in the Celtic script known as ogam and in Irish. The Norse text reads **þurkrim:risti·(k)rusþina**, 'Thorgrímr raised this cross', while the Celtic one has been reconstructed *beandac(h)t (ar) Toreaqr(im)*, 'a blessing on Thorgrímr'. This mixture of Celtic and Norse, and the borrowing of the word *kross* from Celtic into Norwegian we will meet again on the Manx monuments. A second inscription is from Greenmount, co. Louth. This is on a copper-alloy strip, part of a sword-fitting, excavated from a grave-mound. It gives an owner formula. The text is undivided into separate words, **tomnalselshofoþasoerþeta** = *Tomnal selshofoþ a soerþ þeta*, 'Dufnall sealshead owns this sword.'

A slab, elaborately carved with a dragon design and with runes, from St Paul's churchyard, London.

The bone comb-case, found at Lincoln, with Thorfastr's runic advertisement of his skill.

The mixed runic and bookhand legend on the font at Bridekirk, Cumbria, naming Richard who made the font.

'Hart's horn', an inscribed antler from Viking Dublin.

In the 1970s excavators worked on several Viking Age sites near the centre of Dublin. Surprisingly these yielded half a dozen inscriptions on the sort of fugitive materials, wood and bone, that often fail to survive. There was a wooden paddle, a plane, a decorated knife-handle, several bits of bone, ribs and scapulae perhaps of sheep or goats, and a piece of antler. These inscriptions remain largely unpublished and indeed uninterpreted. The paddle has a text which is hard now to make out because of the effect of the treatment to preserve the wood: Aslak Liestøl, the Norwegian runologist, earlier read it **kirlak**, perhaps the personal name *Geirlákr*. Liestøl read a graffito on a rib-bone **onaasu**, and suggested it be divided *Ón á Ásu*, 'Ón is married to Ása.' The most convincing text of this group is that on the antler, which begins **hurn:hiartaR** before tailing off to a broken edge. This means 'hart's horn', which it undoubtedly is, though why it was worth saying I do not know.

The Killaloe and Greenmount texts show the mixing of Norse and Celtic peoples. Even more striking is that shown on the thirty or so runic crosses from the Isle of Man. Most of these are from the central Viking Age, the tenth and eleventh centuries, but there is evidence to show that the script persisted in use into the twelfth. Manx runes show formal links to those of the Norwegian province of Jæren, in the south-west of that country, which suggests a special cultural connection between the two areas. Yet there are occasional cases of Danish runes on the island, and even a mixed inscription, so there was probably a variety of different Viking incomer groups. We have no other records of the Viking settlement of Man, so the rune-stones give valuable information.

They cluster near churches: at Andreas, Braddan, Kirk Michael and Maughold, for instance, and the design of the stone incorporates a cross. The Manx Vikings were probably converted to Christianity before their mainland contemporaries.

The earliest of these runic crosses should be – if you believe what you read in advertisements – one at Kirk Michael which has, after a commemoration formula, the maker's name: **kaut. kirþi: þanᶏ:auk ala:imaun**', 'Gautr made it and all in Man.' I take this to mean that Gautr claimed to be the first maker of inscribed runic crosses in the island (though there was a long tradition of raising cross-stones in the pre-Viking era). Another cross, this time at Andreas, tells a little more about this man: **kautr:kar(þ)i: sunr:biarnar fra:kuli**, 'Gautr, son of Bjǫrn of Kollr, made (this).' These are the only two crosses with his signature, though art historians have attributed others to him on stylistic grounds. Two other rune-cutters are known by name, Árni (Maughold) and Thuríðr (Onchan).

The Manx crosses have a common memorial formula, *N reisti kross þenna eft(ir) M*, 'N put up this cross in memory of M.' To this might be added further details of raiser or commemorated. For instance, the man Sandúlfr who put up a cross at Andreas had the nickname *hinn svarti*, 'the black'. The relationship of the deceased to the raiser is often given – wife, father, son, foster-mother. Sometimes there is additional, moral, comment. At Kirk Michael is a splendid cross-slab with two inscriptions on the back. The first is commemorative, and seems to say – though the grammar is weak – that the cross was raised by a foster-son for his foster-mother. The second is a proverb: 'It is better to leave a good foster-son than a bad son.' At Braddan is a cross fragment, the main inscription of which is lost. All we have is the additional comment showing why the man needed commemoration: 'and Hrossketill betrayed under trust a man sworn to him by oath.' In view of the Vikings' urgent desire for a good report after death, it is ironic that the dead man's name should be lost, but that of the villain who deceived him lives on.

Gautr's cross
at Kirk Michael,
Isle of Man.

The fragmentary cross at
Braddan, Isle of Man,
which tells of the
treacherous Hrossketill
who betrayed his fellow.

The Hunterston brooch
with, to the left of the pin,
the runic owner's
inscription. The symbols to
the right of the pin pretend
to be runes, but are in fact
meaningless.

An important thing about many of these crosses is their suggestion of a multi-racial society, with Norseman marrying Celt. Personal names are not a safe guide to race, yet there are several examples on the Manx stones of families with members with both Norse and Celtic names, and this is surely significant. So, for example, Ófeigr (Norse) was the son of ?Krinan (Celtic) (Braddan); Thorleifr hnakki (Norse) had a son Fiac (Celtic) whose uncle was Hafr (Norse) (Braddan); Aðisl (Norse) married the daughter of Dufgal (Celtic) (Kirk Michael). In one or two cases all the names in the inscription are Celtic, but the language of the text is Norse; but it is Norse with a slight difference, for the word for the monument here is the Celtic loan-word *kross*, not the usual Norwegian word which would be *steinn*, 'stone'. Moreover the Norse is not very good Norse either, for it is full of grammatical irregularities and solecisms. Occasional errors of grammar are not unknown in Norway, but the incidence of them on the Manx stones is very high, and suggests a community speech that has lost its formal precision, perhaps because its users were bilingual. The implication is that in the tenth century Man had a mixed society of Celts and Scandinavians, who intermarried. Since Norse was the official language for public notices, the Vikings were presumably politically dominant.

There were probably similar racial mixtures in Scotland too, though the runes here are fewer and more scattered, and it is unfortunate that most texts are fragmentary so that detailed translation is difficult. At any rate the broken cross from Inchmarnock, Bute, has a memorial formula including that Celtic word *kross*, as does another fragment from Kilbar, Barra. At Hunterston, Strathclyde, was found a fine Celtic-type brooch, with a text in Swedo-Norwegian runes and in Old Norse, but naming a Celt as owner: **malbriþaastilk**, 'Melbrigda owns (this) brooch.'

More consistently Norse are a couple of inscriptions on Scottish grave-slabs, though they vary slightly the wording recorded hitherto. On Iona was found a slab with an engraved interlace cross pattern and the text: **kali·auluis·sunr·laþi·stan·þinsi·ubir·fukl·bruþur·(sin)**, 'Kali Ǫlvissonr laid this stone over his brother Fugl.' A fragmentary inscription on a stone cross laid upon a grave at Thurso says ... **ubirlakþita:aft:ikulb:foþursin**, '... this overlay in memory of Ingólfr his father.'

The Orkneys and Shetlands have stone fragments with runes on them, the remnant of what was clearly a goodly number of memorials. However, the most interesting runic texts from these islands are in the prehistoric stone-built grave-chamber Maeshowe. They are post-Viking, for it seems that the howe was broken into and used as a shelter or meeting-place for Norsemen in the twelfth century. Several cut graffiti on the walls – there are some thirty texts there, and they are not dissimilar to modern graffiti. There are the signatures: 'Vémundr cut (these runes)', 'These runes Úframr Sigurðarsonr cut', 'Hermundr hard-axe cut runes', and so on. There are references to girl-friends: 'Ingibjǫrg the lovely widow', 'Ingigerðr is the loveliest of women.' There is one that looks indelicate, though ambiguous. The mound, says one, was broken into by 'Jerusalem-men', which is to say Crusaders. A group of inscriptions tell a tale of treasure hidden in the burial chamber, a common motif of Old Norse literature. 'It's true what I say, the treasure was moved out of here. The treasure was taken away three days before they broke into the mound.' And a longing one on the same theme: 'Happy the man who can find the great treasure.'

And there is a boasting assertion in a variety of rune forms, an inscription I would like to have cut myself. 'The man who wrote these runes knows more about runes than anyone else west of the sea.'

7
Runes in North America

Several years ago archaeologists identified a Norse settlement, dating from *c*. 1000 AD, at a site at L'Anse-aux-Meadows in the north of Newfoundland, and hailed it as the first unambiguous archaeological evidence for Norsemen in the New World. However, it had long been known, on documentary evidence, that in their voyages of exploration west over the Atlantic some Vikings reached the North American mainland, calling it *Vinland*. Since Vikings used runes, they might be expected to take their script with them across the ocean, so it is not surprising that over many years enthusiastic Americans, particularly those with Scandinavian forebears, sought to find runic inscriptions on their continent. If you look for something single-mindedly enough, you are likely to find it; or at any rate something that looks like it; or at least something that has been made to look like it. This is what happened with American runes.

In 1961 the German scholar Hertha Marquardt published an important bibliography of the runic inscriptions of the British Isles; to it she added an appendix of the reported runic inscriptions of North America. This appendix catalogues finds from some forty distinct sites, and there have been more discoveries since her list came out. They range from New England to the Midwest, from Maine to the Mississippi and to Minnesota. The thing they have in common is that not a single one has yet been accepted as genuinely runic by the professional runologists of Scandinavia. Some have been seen to be natural marks or weathering furrows on rocks; others plough or harrow marks on buried stones; others again, though resembling runes in their general form, are likely to have some other ethnic origin, say Indian; yet others have been rejected as frankly modern inscriptions, or as fakes intended for joke or for deception. For all the scepticism of the Old World, there are still numbers of Americans who wish to demonstrate that one or other of these inscriptions is both runic and genuine.

The difficulty is that such inscriptions, even those clearly meant as runic, look anomalous when compared with genuine material in Scandinavia itself. They have occasional letter forms that are unexampled elsewhere, or are inconsistent with the date attached to the inscription; or they show selections of rune types which, considering the known course of development of the script, could not have existed simultaneously. The language of the text, though containing Norse elements, is often not like that of any known historical period. Find-reports may be confused or disputed. Sometimes even the object is lost, and is known only from early and inexpert report.

The Spirit Pond rune-stones are a case in point. According to report, an amateur antiquary (without archaeological expertise) found them on the banks of the Morse River, near Popham Beach, Phippsburg, Maine, in 1971. The discoverer reported them to the local museum curator, and together they sought expert opinion on the inscriptions with indifferent success. Meanwhile, the state authorities, learning of this find made on state land, demanded the stones, which incensed the finder so much that he reburied them. Eventually, a compromise was reached, and the stones were dug up again and handed to the state museum under conditions. But no subsequent investigation of the supposed find-site uncovered evidence of Vikings. The three carved stones are certainly imposing; particularly so one with a map cut on it, with the runic place-names *Hóp* and *Vínland*, names known to us from the later Icelandic saga of Eric the Red.

The classic American rune-stone is that discovered near Kensington, Minnesota, and now at the county seat, Alexandria. The find-report tells how a Swedish-American farmer, Olof Ohman, was grubbing up trees on his land when he spotted the inscribed stone clasped in the roots of one of them. The find was published in January 1899, and since then fierce strife has raged over the authenticity of this monument with, in general, the Scandinavian runologists – and some of their American colleagues – rejecting it with contumely, and the local patriots defending stoutly.

If it is genuine, it is vastly important. It tells, in Professor Wahlgren's translation: '8 Swedes and 22 Norwegians on an exploration journey from Vinland westward. We had our camp by 2 rocky islets one day's journey north of this stone. We were out fishing one day. When we came home we found 10 men red with blood and dead. AVM save us from evil. We have 10 men by the sea to look after our ships, 14 days' journey from this island. Year 1362.'

It is a stirring story, with the sort of detail about Norsemen in midwest America that is not recorded anywhere else. Only the unimaginative runologist will fail to be impressed. But I have already declared myself an unimaginative runologist.

Below The rune-inscribed map on a stone from Spirit Pond, Maine.

Left The famous, or notorious, rune-stone from Kensington, Minnesota.

8
Where to look for Runes

If you want to look out runes for yourself, the most available collection is in the British Museum – many are on public display – and there are also some in the National Museum of Antiquities of Scotland. Smaller museums often have the local material, as at Lindisfarne and Whithorn, while Durham has the St Cuthbert relics. Some runic monuments remain at or near their original sites. This is obviously the case with the great runic crosses at Bewcastle and Ruthwell, but it also applies to less well-known pieces – the stones of Great Urswick and Thornhill are in their local churches. The Manx stones are scattered through the island, though there are groups of them collected together in the churches of Andreas, Braddan (Old Church), Kirk Michael and, under cover in the churchyard, Maughold.

This cross-shaft, bearing the name *Eadmund* in a mixture of runes and Roman letters, is still at Chester-le-Street. It was found in the walls of the church there during the restorations of 1883.

Bibliographical Note

Of making many books on runes there is no end, but most of them are in German or one of the Scandinavian languages. For those who read French there is an excellent survey of the whole field: Musset, L., *Introduction à la runologie* (Paris, 1965). In English there is Elliott, R. W. V., *Runes: an introduction* (Manchester, 1959, reprinted). A recent volume of individual studies reports the proceedings of the First International Symposium on Runes and Runic Inscriptions, and forms Volume VII (1981) of *Michigan Germanic Studies*.

The Scandinavian countries have taken their runes seriously, and have published, or are in the process of publishing, complete corpora of runic monuments. For Denmark there is a very good general study in Moltke, E., *Runes and their origin: Denmark and elsewhere* (Copenhagen, 1985). This gives a complete account of the Danish runic monuments as they have survived, and also contains important observations on the origins and development of the script and the problems of interpretation. For Sweden there is an interesting introductory book, though it mainly concerns itself with the Viking Age rune-stones, Jansson, S. B. F., *The runes of Sweden* (London, 1962).

The Anglo-Saxon runes are summarised in my *An introduction to English runes* (London, 1973). For the Scandinavian runes in the British Isles the general reader will have to go back to Shetelig, H. (ed.), *Viking antiquities in Great Britain and Ireland*, VI (Oslo, 1954) which has a survey article by the great Norwegian runologist Magnus Olsen, though it is now somewhat outdated. I surveyed the Manx runes in an article in Fell, C. E. and others (eds), *The Viking Age in the Isle of Man* (London, 1983).

Index